THIS IS YOUR
CAPTAN
SPEAKING

Reaching for the Sky
Despite a Lifetime of Abuse, Depression and Fear

COURTNEY SCHOCH

Published in Cleveland, Ohio, by Courtney Schoch LLC.

Books may be available for bulk purchase for educational, business, fund-raising, or sales promotional use. For information, please contact the publisher at:

Courtney Schoch, LLC.
7801 Day Drive, #29477
Cleveland, Ohio 44129

Or email:
courtney@courtneyschoch.com

Some names and identifying details have been changed to protect the privacy of individuals. All conversations have been re-created to the best of the author's memory. This book only presents the author's perspective.

Due to the content and subject matter, this book is intended for a mature audience.

Printed in the United States of America

ISBN-13 (print): 978-1-7348935-4-0
ISBN-13 (ebook): 978-1-7348935-7-1

Library of Congress Control Number: 2020906682

Publishing Services provided by TKI Publishing, LLC. at www.tkipublishing.com
Editorial Service provided by Lisa Thompson at www.writebylisa.com

DEDICATION

For those struggling to find meaning—it's there. I promise.

TABLE OF CONTENTS

ACKNOWLEDGMENTS

———————◆———————

Katherine Brown: I love you for being you. Everything happened the way it was supposed to. You taught me to be strong, and now so many will be inspired because of you.

Zachary Lach: You've been the only stable man in my life. Thank you for the love and support. You've done an incredible job despite many challenges and I know you will continue to do so. I'm proud of you. You've got this! I love you.

Gabriella Schoch: You inspired me to speak up for women of all ages. Watching you grow over the years into a strong, courageous woman who puts good into the world makes me smile. I love you. Keep moving forward. XOXO

1

Caroline Membreño: You commented on my Facebook page, and here it is! You named my first book. Thank you! I extend much gratitude and love to you for supporting my journey and being a true friend.

TKI Publishing: Without your guidance, professionalism, support, patience, suggestions, and encouragement, this book might have lived in my head forever. Thank you for making the book-writing experience exciting, fun, and informative.

Jessica Salazar: You are the best coach a girl could have. You've taught me many things in the last year. The most important lesson is to keep moving forward: action creates confidence. Thank you. I'm doing FANTASTIC!

Eric Brown: Thank you for giving me the courage to leap and not let me fall apart. Even though I did at times.

ProLiteracy, Michele Bellso, and Kevin Morgan: You took a chance on me in San Diego and gave me a platform to reach so many. I am forever grateful. Thank you.

Amanda Iacona: Thank you for finding the energy after a hard workout to share your input on the book cover, subtitles, and other ideas. And for saving my cat Ollie.

Katie Kucera: You set the bar high as my first marketing master. Thank you. You're awesome, and because of you, I will forever be known by many adult learners as the "Running with Lions Lady."

Social media friends and supporters: Your likes, comments, shares, and support provided the emotional momentum I needed to get through the rough spots in my writing process. Love you all! Thank you.

INTRODUCTION

The wind is whipping my auburn curly hair around my face as I sit in the backseat of a 1969 pumpkin-orange Dodge Charger. The car accelerates through the hot sticky summer night in Atlanta onto I-75, the main interstate that runs through Georgia. As my feet tap to the beat of John Fogerty's "Fortunate Son" on the radio, I color Wonder Woman's golden magic lasso in my superhero coloring book.

Gunshots suddenly shatter the night; I look up just in time as my father puts the shiny black handgun on top of the dashboard. A wood-paneled station wagon spins out of control, sparks trailing the bumper as metal scrapes across the pavement. The vehicle comes to an abrupt stop in the grass on the side of the highway. *What just happened?* I think. *Did Dad just shoot out the man's car tires? Why? Maybe that bad man had cut him off.* I shrug and gaze down at the coloring book and begin to search the Crayola Crayon box for the perfect shade of red to color Wonder Woman's knee-high boots.

This was one of my earliest childhood memories at age five. Events like this were my normal and would shape the perspective and experiences into my adulthood. As a child, nothing about life then seemed abnormal to me, but as I grew older, I learned that these destructive patterns must be broken to pave a path to self-empowerment and eventually end the drama my life would become.

SECTION ONE
GEORGIA

CHAPTER 1

A New Mom

———————◆————————

"Do you want a bunny?" my dad asked as we walked through the woods on a gravel path alongside the rippling waters of the Chattahoochee River. The tree leaves were covered in dew, and the morning air was thick with the smell of freshly cut grass. The ground crunched with each step we took.

Did Dad check me out of school right after my first period class to surprise me with a bunny? Or did he find an injured bunny nearby and want to save it by bringing it home? He loves animals and often stops driving to park on the side of the road so he can scoop up innocent creatures that had been hit and flattened by cars. He then places them on the grass so that cars do not keep running over them. I wonder what he's up to?

"Sure, but what will Mom say?" I asked. "Bunnies are messy," I added. I remember learning that they chewed on clothes, cords, table legs, and anything else they could sink their buck teeth into.

"Your *new* mom loves bunnies, and she will give you a bunny if you like her. Then we will live together. Wouldn't you like to have a bunny? You've always wanted one."

New mom? What did Dad mean? What was wrong with the mom I had now? At just seven years old, as far as I was aware, my mommy was at home cleaning the house, cooking dinner, and working three jobs so that we could have nice things. That's what she always said she was doing: working day and night so we could have nice things. She was doing everything a good mommy should do, so why did we need a new one?

While my young brain was trying to process what my dad had just said about a new mom, a tall, willowy woman suddenly stepped out of the woods onto the path where my dad and I stood. Her high heels sank deep into the ground, disappearing into the gravel as she walked toward us. Her long, straight blonde hair shimmered in the sunlight, and her warm eyes and tan flawless smooth skin reminded me of the color of toast. As she bent down to hug me, her silky white shirt slid across my cheek and her perfume smelled like a chocolate fudge sundae with rainbow sprinkles.

Then my dad looked into my blue eyes and stated firmly yet sincerely, "This is Diane. I want her to be your new mom. She loves you."

"Okay," I eagerly replied without hesitation. "I would like a bunny and a new mom."

How exciting! Something new. I knew my old mom was unhappy and complained about all the jobs she had to work because of my dad and his stupid get-rich-quick schemes. I just knew she would be happy Dad found someone else so she wouldn't have to keep doing everything.

As I continued to spend time with them, my new mom laughed and joked with my dad as they walked hand in hand on the path. Her silky white shirt, linen pants, and classy high heels contrasted with the clothes my old mom wore: a scratchy polyester blend, depending on which job she was working. My dad stroked her hair, and she smiled. I couldn't remember the last time my old mom smiled.

I bet Diane has a huge mansion. She probably has a maid that speaks Spanish, wears a white crisp uniform with a bow, and keeps everything sparkling clean, I thought. My sun-kissed, freckled face beamed as I stood on my tiptoes to give my new mom a big hug again. I just knew that if I held onto her tightly enough, she would stay forever.

We spent the morning into the early afternoon together walking, laughing and skipping rocks on the river shore. Then dad surprised us with a picnic. The red-and-white checkered blanket and wicker basket were already set up in an open, spacious grassy area. Nearby willow trees provided shade in case it got too hot. The basket was full of different types of cubed cheeses, water crackers, red seedless grapes, and miniature chocolate eclairs. *A small feast!* After lunch, I hugged Diane goodbye. Dad told me I could start walking to the car, and he would catch up. He stayed behind to talk a little longer with Diane before he ran to the car to meet me.

On the drive home, we chatted the whole way about our new future and our new family. We dreamed about the days to come. I skipped up the paved driveway which led to the crooked front wooden stairs and burst into the front door. I tossed my Strawberry Shortcake backpack onto the black leather couch, kicked off my sandals and began to tell my mom all about Diane. As I shared the events of the day, her demeanor suddenly changed. She frowned, and her hazel eyes flooded with tears in an unexpected but familiar storm of emotions. Darkness filled her eyes.

Just then, my dad walked through the front door. The hurt that just moments ago had shown on my mother's face quickly turned to rage at my father's presence. My mother yelled, "Son of a bitch," and the insults tossed back and forth between them for what felt like forever. As their voices rose, my insides twisted into a knot, as if I were at an amusement park. Similar to the feeling you have right before being strapped in the hard plastic seat on a roller coaster and you have no idea what will happen next. This moment was much like that. I could sense what was coming: a fight.

I slipped down the hall into my bedroom, shut the door, and sat crisscross applesauce in the small closet. A pillow, blanket, and flashlight were already in the closet. I pretended that I was on a secret mission. I pulled out my diary and started thinking of a name for my new bunny.

Frequently the police or a neighbor showed up when my parents fought. I anticipated it would not take long to hear a loud knock on the front door. Sometimes the response was delayed for days after a fight had ended. As I sat looking at a sliver of light underneath the closet door, I remembered last year when two police officers and a social worker showed up at our house. A concerned neighbor had contacted the local authorities. They swiftly led me to my small bedroom and inspected my body for bruises. I had several that had faded in color from angry purple to pale yellow. Instead of arresting or admonishing my parents, they strolled past them on the way to the front door and the officers casually told my mom that more parents should discipline their children in the same way because it made their job easier.

The screams and sounds of fists hitting flesh brought me back to the present moment. They distracted me occasionally, but I tried

13

to ignore them. Instead I concentrated on the bunny's name. I was deep in thought when suddenly, *thud!* Someone—probably my mom—slammed into the wall. My dad had likely thrown or shoved her. Then a new noise. *Thump, thump, thump!* My face beamed with pride. *Success!* The sound inspired my bunny's name, Thumper. Eventually the fighting stopped and I fell asleep on top of my green flannel blanket and dreamed of my new room in the mansion, the maid's crisp uniform, and Diane's shiny hair.

When I woke up the next morning, my mom was in the kitchen cooking grits and scrambled eggs for me before I headed off to school, and my dad wasn't home.

After days of waiting, there was no new mom, no maid, and no Thumper. My dad and mom had been getting along better since the day in the park. I thought maybe it had been a test—the woman, the picnic, the bunny—to see if I passed. I don't think I did because my mom had stopped talking to me. She always commented about my weight or about how frizzy my hair was and now she ignored me. I knew I shouldn't have told her about Diane. It was a secret, but I couldn't keep quiet. I convinced myself that I always messed up and made my parents mad. *That's okay. I'll have another chance to make things better, there will be another test. There always is.*

Six months later, we moved into a new house, the third move in three years. I had stopped unpacking all of the cardboard boxes two years earlier. *Why get comfortable?* My dad told me his job as

14

a private investigator was dangerous and that the bad guys might find out where we live and want to hurt us. We had to move around to stay safe. I understood that Dad wanted to protect me and remembered what had happened last summer when we lived in the apartment by the lake.

We were at the neighborhood playground with another little girl. While playing, she began to stomp on my tennis shoes. I asked her to stop but she didn't listen and the mud on the bottom of her shoe was starting to darken the white laces of mine. As she stomped she called me names. My dad approached her, whispered something in her ear, and then twisted her tiny ankle while she sat on the swing. I heard a snap. He had broken it. He lifted me high on his shoulders and we walked away. I never saw that girl on the playground again. My mom was upset when she heard what had happened but knew my dad was friends with the local authorities and they would not prosecute him.

Mom told me, "Your dad is a good man and didn't mean to do it. He just loses his temper sometimes because he loves us so much and can't control himself. It is just like when he hits us, but we have to remember that families stick together. No matter what."

CHAPTER 2

Families Stick Together

———————◆———————

L ight illuminated the small bedroom, waking up both my half-sister, Jennifer, and me. My mom had flipped on the light switch to tell us that she was leaving soon. She already had on her knee-length sweater coat and shoes. Uncle Stephen had died, she matter of factly informed us, and she needed to leave for the hospital immediately as soon as she received the call. *How did she know if no one had called yet?*

Jennifer slept over at our house once a month and was one of two children from my dad's previous marriage. She rolled her eyes at my mother, a common response, and Jennifer and I exchanged uncertain glances. Perhaps the unidentifiable feeling was due to the abrupt waking or disbelief at the situation and at her words. I'd never had someone close to me die. Neither of us believed her because her reasoning was bizarre, and she was unusually calm.

The sharp ring of the rotary kitchen phone cut through the house at two o'clock in the morning. An eerie quiet fell as my mom walked out of our bedroom to answer it. She murmured a few hushed words and hung up. She walked out the front door with my dad without a word. Three hours later, we learned the details. Uncled Stephen had committed suicide by combining Maalox with a bottle of aspirin and washing it down with Mad Dog. My mom had given us news moments earlier.

Stephen was the younger of my dad's two brothers. He lived an isolated life in his bedroom in my grandparent's home. He did not have friends or a job and usually slept the entire day. He reminded me of a mysterious vampire with many secrets.

No one suspected anything was wrong until the day he killed himself. We later learned he had been charged with a DUI hours earlier, but no one even knew he drank. My family believed that Stephen had returned home after being bailed out of jail by my grandfather to implement his suicide plan while his parents ate lunch at their favorite restaurant. He went to his room and disposed of his porn stash along with a dozen empty vodka bottles. He stuffed it all in a black plastic bag and took it to the curb for trash collection. My father discovered the bags the day after he died. My grandparents avoided going back to the house after they left the hospital for as long as possible to delay the reality of the suicide and instead visited friends. My mom and dad cleaned up my uncle's room to minimize the shock and grief when my grandparents returned.

Before and after Uncle Stephen died, I spent much of my childhood at my grandparents' brick ranch home near the Atlanta airport. My grandparents' rarely spoke to each other in my presence and I never saw them show any affection toward each other. They married when my grandmother was a rising radio singer in Chattanooga after World War II. She was taking care of her mother, my great-grandmother Mimi, a decorated and respected Red Cross nurse. They needed someone to financially provide for them, and my grandfather came along at just the right time. He agreed to their monetary stipulations in exchange for marriage. My grandmother was only intimate with my grandfather often enough to become pregnant, according to her. She disclosed intimate details of her relationship with my mother but never with me. My grandmother shared innocent stories and juicy neighborhood or celebrity gossip when we sat at the kitchen table playing card games she taught me. I spent a lot of time at my grandparent's house because she babysat me when my mom and dad were working. My mom would also suggest a sleepover at their house when she anticipated a fight at home.

During these visits, which sometimes lasted for days, my grandmother and I shared her king-sized bed and binge watched

Dark Shadows TV episodes in her room. We loved to read. We would lie on her bed, engrossed in a great mystery novel for hours. When we were ready to take a break, she'd whip up a meal consisting of scrambled eggs, chipped beef, toast, and spicy V-8 juice.

Uncle Stephen was quiet. His bedroom was at the end of the long hall next to the bathroom. The bedroom had heavy cherry wood furniture set against burgundy walls. The ranch-style home had three bedrooms, one small bathroom near the hallway entrance to the kitchen, a dining room, a living room, and a den. My grandparents had separate bedrooms, and Stephen occupied the remaining room.

We connected when I saw him. Although I spent a lot of time at my grandparents' home, he stayed in his room, so I didn't see him often. We played board games, charades, and he would tell funny jokes. I could never remember the jokes, but I always laughed so hard that my stomach muscles ached and tears of laughter streamed down my cheeks.

CHAPTER 3

Secrets and Lies

———————◆———————

M y father, Walter, was born outside Atlanta and was always a bit of a rebel. My grandfather was a strong disciplinarian and took his marital frustrations out on my dad. Walter's southern charm and irresponsible behavior resulted in a girl's pregnancy during high school when he was seventeen. After learning of the pregnancy, he reluctantly drove to South Carolina with the girl where they married. She was his first wife. The state of Georgia required a blood test, and my father was terrified of needles, so he decided to get married in another state that did not require a test. That marriage resulted in the addition of one more child two years later, a daughter, Jennifer.

They divorced three years later. Walter followed his passion and joined a band, playing bass guitar. Throughout his life, he drifted in and out of low-paying jobs, including as a pest exterminator, radioactive material transporter and a security guard. Sometimes he would work in the grocery store my grandfather owned to make money, but his parents often carried his financial burdens, including paying child support to his first wife. For years, my grandfather resented spending so much money on him. My grandfather had many regrets. He often shared his biggest regret with us. The story of how he declined an opportunity to partner with his friend Truett Cathy in a neighborhood restaurant idea that would later be known as Chick-fil-A.

My mother, Irene, was born in Indianapolis. She was the second oldest of four siblings and became pregnant when she was a junior in high school. Her mother was overly critical and rarely supportive. Her father, in contrast, was gentle and cerebral, working as a school teacher. Irene did not marry the father of her son, Lee, but she married twice before the age of twenty-three. Each marriage lasted less than a year, and with each husband, she hoped to find a father figure for her son. She worked in a division of the Army, inputting data as a civilian, and also as a waitress to support herself and Lee.

My parents met when my father was playing a band gig in Indianapolis and my mother was waitressing at the same tiny smoke-filled corner bar. She was twenty-four and he was twenty-three. Six months after meeting my father, my mother moved to Atlanta, leaving her six-year-old son to live with her parents. She had hoped Lee would later join her in Atlanta, but once she realized how violent my father was, she opted to have her parents, my grandparents, legally adopt him.

Two years after their courtship, I was conceived, and my parents legally married when I was four years old. They took yet another drive to South Carolina to avoid a blood test. I was raised as an only child and met my half-brother, Lee, once or twice during my childhood. I had limited exposure to Eric and Jennifer even though they lived nearby. My parents were both busy building their private investigator business, and my mother worked numerous jobs to provide medical benefits for us and to cover the expenses my dad incurred while seducing numerous women.

One rainy fall day, my grandparents left in their autumn gold Chevrolet station wagon to go to a doctor's appointment. I was in the house with Uncle Stephen, curled up on my grandmother's bed, reading a Nancy Drew mystery novel. The villain was about to be revealed, but I had to pee and couldn't hold it any longer. I hopped up and rushed down the hallway to the bathroom. Stephen unexpectedly stepped out of his room right into my path. I was shy and did not want him to hear me. Instead of going straight into the bathroom, I veered to the right into the kitchen to get a glass of water from the refrigerator's dispenser. I pretended to sip it in case he was watching me. Once I felt comfortable and assumed he was no longer watching, I hurried to the bathroom. Just as I was about to shut the door, his door abruptly opened again. He extended his arm and pushed on the bathroom door, keeping it from closing.

"I need to get something," he said.

"Okay," I replied. My stomach dropped as a strange dread grew within me. But at the time, I had no idea why his behavior seemed off. I forgot I had to pee.

He stepped into the tiny bathroom decorated with ceramic tiles on the walls and floor—all the same color: daisy yellow. He closed the door behind him and locked it. *Click.* Now I really knew something was wrong, but I didn't know what to say. I was ten years old and locked in a tiny bathroom that smelled of lemon Lysol with my twenty-six-year-old uncle.

He stood between me and the door, unzipped his pants, and pulled out his penis. I didn't know what to do. I'd only seen a man naked once before and that was when I woke up in the middle of the night the previous year and saw my dad drinking out of the milk carton, the refrigerator interior light illuminating his body.

"Touch it, just once. You know you want to," Uncle Stephen told me.

I just stood there, paralyzed. I thought of a trapped animal, the kind I saw on the National Geographic TV shows. I scanned the bathroom, looking in vain for an escape. One small window near the shower overlooked the patio. My mind searched for answers as to what was happening. He was my *uncle*. I thought he was my friend. We laughed together at silly jokes, and he teased me because my hair looked like an afro in the humid Atlanta summers. *Why was he asking me to touch him?*

I stopped asking myself questions, my mind blank until the warmth spread down my legs, soaking my shorts. I started crying as I peed on myself. Something shifted in my uncle, and his face softened. He reached behind him and unlocked the door, opened it, backed up into his bedroom, his pants still unzipped and shut his door.

I ran through the house into the backyard, past my grandfather's tomato garden, and collapsed on a tree stump by the neglected pet graves near the sun bleached wooden swinging bench. My wet shorts were sticking to me as I pulled my knees in closer to my body, and I breathed in relief as the rain washed away the urine and shame. My mother's voice echoed inside my head, a recording on repeat. The words blurred and ran together in my mind. "Families stick together no matter what. Families stick together no matter what. Families stick together no matter what." I knew I would not tell anyone what had happened and pass the test this time. I suppressed the experience and kept the secret until I was forty-three years old.

CHAPTER 4

A Better Version of Me

———————◆———————

At an early age, I taught myself that not asking questions allowed the storm to pass more quickly. The first place I'd go whenever we moved to a new home was to the bedroom closet. That was the portal to my secret world—where I'd write, hide, and dream of a better life. Life was easier when I used my imagination to retreat to a fantasyland of my choosing than to live in the present moment. I could be a superhero saving the world, strong, fierce, and admired by all—or a scientist who finds black holes to travel to a new world or discovers hidden wormholes on Earth.

I had very few friends because my family relocated so often and I had lost the ability to trust others. It was challenging to establish relationships, and sometimes, when I did, I may have been better off not trying. On a cloudless July day, when I was ten, my friend Michele invited me to ride bicycles around our neighborhood. The surrounding area was full of rolling hills, and each one took tremendous effort to climb. The silver handlebar tassels slapped against my knuckles with the warm breeze. We were three blocks from Michele's house, and she was riding in front of me. She motioned with her hand, indicating that she wanted us to ride toward her house. My leg muscles strained and my lungs burned as I pedaled fast and furious against the wind, trying to keep up with her. The downhill slope of the street helped, and I coasted to a stop in front of her garage door. We propped our bikes against the red brick house and walked into the cool basement. I was not allowed into anyone's house without my parents' permission, but I thought it was safe this one time because my mom had Michele's phone number and she knew I was with her.

Michele told me to wait while she went upstairs to the kitchen to get us grape popsicles. Her brother, Larry, slipped silently through the same door we had just entered. The creaky door hinge gave him away. *He's sneaky and creepy, and what is he hiding? A rifle!* Before I knew what was happening, he grabbed me by my hair and dragged me upstairs to his bedroom. He shut the door and engaged the lock. My heart pounded, threatening to escape my body. But I didn't make a sound and hoped Michele would get help. As she called my name, her footfalls grew louder as she ascended the stairs from the basement to the second floor.

Silent, I sat and stared at the muzzle of Larry's rifle. He sat with his back against the wall for hours. The sun began to set, and the room darkened. Michele pounded on the bedroom door and told her brother to open it. Larry ignored her. He never spoke a word. My voice stuck in my throat, and I stared at a large freckle on my right arm. *Is each cell in my body aware of this situation? Does each one exist in its world, oblivious to what's happening? Is there an alternate universe where I'm sitting outside eating a grape popsicle next to my bicycle?*

If I tried hard enough, I could escape my current reality and pretend this was not happening. My mother often reminded me how I'd crawl underneath a glass-topped coffee table in the living room and color when I was younger. I'd pretend as if I were in a secret world that no one knew about. It didn't matter that I was hiding under clear glass and everyone else could see me. I created my perception of the event inside my head. I disconnected from reality, choosing to create my own.

Now, I used the same technique in Larry's bedroom. A familiar voice finally came from the other side of the door. It was my mother. Larry jumped, and he quickly hid the rifle under the mattress, yanked me up by my arm, unlocked the door, and shoved me, directly into my mother. Both of us stumbled onto the hallway floor. She grabbed my hand and rushed me down the stairs and out the door into her white Nissan minivan. We drove away and I watched my favorite bike, abandoned on the side of the house, disappear from view as we turned the street corner.

My mom had called Michele's home number several times with no answer when I did not show up to dinner. She found the address in the phone book and drove over to the house. No one answered the door, but she saw my bike and walked into the house. Michele was frantically attempting to wake up her mother, who was passed out on the couch reeking of alcohol. Michele told my mom that she thought I was in her brother's room, and my mom rushed up the stairs to rescue me.

We never told my father what happened, and I never saw Michele, her family or my bike again.

Sometimes I wished I had my older brothers, Eric and Lee, around to protect me from the bullies at school and at home. When Eric turned eighteen, he joined the Navy, and I did not reconnect with him until I was thirty-two. Lee had gotten into trouble with theft and drug abuse and had been incarcerated since he was seventeen. I would not see him again for more than thirty years, when I visited him at a Missouri maximum-security prison with our mom. We would never again reconnect as a family unit. Everyone lived their individual lives. We were strangers with DNA as the only common denominator.

CHAPTER 5

Twist and Turns

———◆———

As I grew older, I paid attention to the extra weight and angry red stretch marks that were starting to appear on my hips and thighs. My mom made hurtful comments whenever I looked bloated or if my clothing did not look just right to her. She struggled with her own weight, and her quest to be thin was never-ending.

The slender models and actresses glared back at me with their hollow eyes from the covers of magazines, silently pleading with me to do something about my hideous appearance. The magazines sat on shelves alongside the candy bars in the grocery store checkout line. I always chose the candy bars, the crunchy chocolate wafer of a Kit Kat was my favorite. My mom preferred the *Enquirer* or any magazine with the newest diet fad on the cover. Once home, she would place them neatly on our living room coffee table as a continuous reminder of what I should strive to be.

Months later, my clothes stopped fitting me, and we couldn't afford new ones, so I made a decision to lose weight. I flipped wildly through magazines for the perfect diet that I could hide from my mom. I did not want her to know. I wanted this to be my choice and not have her criticize me when I messed it up.

As I shuffled through the magazine pages, my eyes fell on a girl with brown curly hair like me, her hip bones protruding from underneath her jeans. *That's the body I want.* It was a simple weight-loss plan called "the popcorn diet," and all I had to do was substitute two meals a day with plain air-popped popcorn. *I can do this*, I thought. The next day, I started the diet, and although I felt as if I were starving every day, I taped the model's image inside my closet door as motivation. She smiled at me every morning, and her smile reminded me that I could be happy and desired like her.

The pounds began to melt away, and I looked forward to stepping on the scale. In six weeks, twenty pounds had disappeared. I was beginning to see my own hip bones and my facial features were more defined. In two months, the new year would arrive, and I planned on losing another twenty-five pounds. My weight goal was one hundred and ten pounds, just right for my five-foot, seven-inch height. Being thinner meant my classmates would have less to tease me about. My clothing would finally fit perfectly when I became lean like Brooke Shields or Christie Brinkley and then my mom would stop criticizing my appearance.

The perfect body shape was defined by the inner thighs not touching each other, a flat stomach, and the outline of rib bones without sucking in. There were no rolls of squishy fat if you bent forward and touched your toes and no jiggle to the underarm flesh. I was on my way to the ideal body! As I became thinner, I gained more confidence and made the connection between beauty and power. Next up was a technique to tame my curly frizzy hair.

I was a sophomore in high school when I experienced my first boyfriend. JP was a senior from my high school with a bad temper. We met during lunch. I was hiding between cars in the student parking lot while smoking, and he was skipping class, sitting in his truck. But he eventually broke up with me just a few weeks after we began dating because I wouldn't have sex with him. We had spent countless make-out sessions in the front of his truck on the bench seat, but I wouldn't go further with him and kept telling him no. I was worried that he would talk to his friends at school about what we did. One day, he left me on the side of the road with an ultimatum: "Put out or walk home." He drove off with a honk, a middle finger out the window, and squealing tires. Before this, he drove me home from school, but I eventually realized that was an excuse for steamy make-out time in his truck. After we ended our relationship, he stopped giving me rides and I had to walk home.

The busy street on my route home from school was filled with traffic: local business delivery trucks, yellow school buses and the vehicles of high school students with their loud blaring music. It was a sunny warm afternoon and the faint smell of asphalt hung in the air, the residual odor from the road crew that had completed repairs the previous week. At the smell, memories of the cat calls directed at me from the workers surfaced. I'd walk by them, rushing to escape their embarrassing whistles.

Suddenly, heat flooded my body and I stopped walking. For a moment, I was confused as the heat intensified. My heart began to race, and hot searing pain gripped my upper thigh. My hip felt as if it were on fire. I was gasping for breath, struggling to stand, let alone to make it home. Then a shout came from the street. JP's dark blue Ford Jimmy pickup truck with the rifle mount and Confederate flag bumper sticker sped by. His words yelled in my direction were lost in the thunderous roar of the engine.

I tried not to limp, but the pain was unbearable. I needed to get home. Humiliation prevented me from asking for help. My eyes remained focused straight ahead until I reached the driveway and looked down. *Why, oh why did I even look?* Fear gripped me at the horrific sight. My stone-washed Jordache jeans were covered in blood, and I knew my mom would be furious. As I stumbled up the driveway, barely making it into the house, my mother caught a glimpse of me. In a frantic panic at the sight of all that blood and my tears, she immediately rushed me to the local emergency room.

I was relieved when the examination of my injury was finally over. The doctor had used a pair of trauma shears to cut my jeans and panties off, leaving me naked from the waist down. After the exam, the emergency-room doctor told us that the damage was from a BB gun. The small metallic ball projectile had sliced through my jeans and the skin near my hip but did not inflict serious damage. When the doctors and police asked me if I knew who had shot me, I lied and told them I had no idea. In my heart, I knew that if I told them, JP would try to shoot me again. And the next time, he would shoot to kill. So I kept quiet.

After the incident, my only friend, Tanya, suggested getting a job so I could buy my own car when I got my license. She worked at a Pizza Hut in the mall. She didn't know that I was only fourteen, too young to be hired. When I first met her, we attended the same middle school, two years ago. At the time, I lied to her about my age because I wanted her to like me, so she thought I was a year older than I really was. I considered telling her the truth, but I knew that if I did, she would feel betrayed, and I'd lose our friendship. I chose to continue living the lie.

In the middle of a lazy, hot, sunny afternoon, we both lay on our stomachs on her gray, itchy basement berber carpet in our stone washed denim shorts and tank tops. We wore our bathing suits underneath because we were planning to go swimming in her subdivision pool after we finished playing PlayStation's Super Mario Brothers. I couldn't swim but pretended to know how. I planned on using the excuse of perfecting my underwater handstand to avoid the deep end of the pool.

"Pizza Hut is hiring. Want me to get you an interview? Linda, the manager, sucks but we would get to work together and hang out all the time," Tanya enthusiastically told me. Then she added, "And you need wheels. I'm tired of driving you around."

"Sure!" I replied and started daydreaming about the red convertible Mazda Miata I would buy with my money. When I left her house, I hurried home, still thinking about my first job.

The following day, Tanya handed me a work application. I started to fill it out, but a section asked for a work permit and stated a required minimum age of fifteen. I remembered that Tanya didn't know my real age. Even so, I wanted this job. I needed it. I sat and thought about how to solve this dilemma and eventually came up with a plan.

I arrived home and found my birth certificate in a desk drawer. I neatly folded it up and rushed to the local office supply store to make copies. Afterwards, I returned home and used my mom's typewriter to change my birth year. It took me several tries to change the "4" to a "2" because the "2" key kept striking higher than the others. After at least five tries at changing the year,

I decided to type in the month, day, and year instead of just typing in the single digit. I'd only made seven copies of my birth certificate at the store, and I was starting to run low.

Finally, after three hours of manipulation, the birth certificate looked official. Since Pizza Hut only needed a copy, not the original, I crinkled up the doctored paper to make it look worn. I hurried back to the office supply store and ran it through the Xerox machine again. Now the entire document looked distressed and took the focus off my birth date and that pesky changed number. Confidently, I took the application and birth certificate to the food court in the mall where Pizza Hut was located and turned it into the shift manager the following day.

A week passed, and I didn't hear any response from Pizza Hut. I started to worry that management could tell that the birth certificate was altered. *What if they knew I was a liar? I was a fake?* Finally, two weeks later the manager called. Linda interviewed and hired me on the spot over the phone. Three days later, I started working my first job.

I excitedly told my parents I was hired, but I didn't tell them that I lied on the application and altered my birth certificate. I figured it wasn't a big deal. They were wrapped up in their own lives and drama, too busy to pay attention to mine. When I needed to work, I'd either hitch a ride with Tanya or one of my parents would drive me. I was so excited to be working. I proudly displayed my red-collared shirt and Pizza Hut visor every shift I was scheduled. The excitement lasted for a while until eventually the job lost its allure and the heavy aroma of pizza dough and pepperoni started to nauseate me.

It was a breezy, cool night, a week before school started. I was working a double shift. I had walked outside for a smoke break. As I stood near the entrance doors to the mall, an older, balding man sauntered up to me and asked for a light. I was leery but willing to oblige, so I gave him one. We started talking as we both took long drags off our Marlboros.

He immediately began to tell me how pretty I was, complimenting my dyed frizzy hair and slim figure. I gave a silent thank-you to the creator of the popcorn diet. After we were done smoking, I walked with him to his van, and before I knew what was happening, I was in the back. He was kissing me—hard and fast, desperately. His hand aggressively moved up my shirt and grabbed my breasts. The Pizza Hut name-tag pin was jamming into my skin. *I do not want to be here. I do not know this man. I'm in the back of his black van with dark tinted windows. What if he tries to do more than put his hand up my shirt?* At the scary thought, I mentally checked out and took a trip to my fantasyland where I was safe. *This is happening to someone else.*

My wristwatch alarm beeped loudly, cutting sharply into the night and transporting me back to the present. It saved me; my break was over, and it was time to go. I straightened my clothes and stumbled out of the van. It had started to rain, and I was grateful that I had an excuse for my streaked makeup and damp hair as I clocked back in from my break and tied the red apron around my waist.

CHAPTER 6

Take Me Away

———————————◆———————————

After the parking-lot incident with the creepy older man in the van, I felt tainted. A sense of shame that could not be shaken permeated my soul as if I had crossed an imaginary emotional boundary, a line that could never be redrawn. I shuddered as memories flooded my brain, creating a veil of abashment: the crack of the BB gun and the moistness of jeans saturated with blood after JP shot me with a BB gun; the despair of being held hostage by Michele's brother in his room with a rifle; the attempted assault by my Uncle Stephen; the many men I'd allowed myself to be intimate with in some form; and more. The list seemed endless.

I often asked myself, *What is good in this life?* The simple answer I heard in replay was "a closet, a stuffed bear named Richie, and my diary." This question was often followed by, *Why can't I live a normal life?* For years, as a young girl, my brain came up with this logical answer: *Because you aren't good enough. If you were, people would treat you better and the fighting would stop.*

I concluded that I was unworthy to have people treat me the way magazines and movies portray normal people. Those families did not punch, yell obscenities, cheat, manipulate, or break a young girl's ankle on the playground. They had meaningful conversations during dinner at the dining room table and played board games while sipping cups of steamy hot chocolate capped with frothy marshmallows. The women had boyfriends who called daily and showed up unexpectedly at the front door with roses. They had a gaggle of close friends who supported each other, gossiping as they sat on the floor painting each other's nails.

My parents' fighting intensified, and I withdrew by partying as a way of coping. The bedroom closet was no longer enough to provide the escape I desperately needed, and writing out my thoughts brought on more depression. Putting my fragmented life in words felt like a dull razor blade slicing through my soul with each pencil stroke. So I erased the painful words until there was nothing left on the paper. I began to seek solace elsewhere, often in the arms of predatory older men in hopes of expunging my past.

I turned into a slut—my own words and description—and my temperament changed from calm to quick anger. At sixteen and seventeen, I slept around with many older men to satisfy the adrenaline rush, the constant craving for attention, and to distract myself.

My fake driver's license allowed me to breeze past bouncers at the coolest clubs in trendy Buckhead, and I became a master of hooking a man, seducing him, and moving on weeks later. I had just enough time to make an escape so that they did not have an opportunity to learn much about me. Most knew me by the name on my fake ID: Melinda.

My idea of fun was in the form of toxic dead-end relationships. I regularly hung out in the apartments of men lacking in character and played drinking games. I spun the story into one that made me feel better and pretended my life was on a fast track to somewhere amazing. I told myself this lie as I walked to my dented, decade old silver Dodge Colt so many mornings after a night with whatever man I had been with, smelling of booze and sex.

Life at home hadn't changed and, in fact, grew worse. My dad crossed the line again and began having an affair with my mom's best friend, Sally. She used to come to our home to visit with my mom. My mom did not have many friends, so I thought this relationship was healthy for her. I was not a fan of Sally because she often asked me to smoke pot with her and always tried to buddy up with me. I had no interest in being her friend. She was an eccentric woman with a heavyset figure embraced in tight spandex. She proudly wore feathers in her hair secured with joint clips and accents of big clunky turquoise jewelry. She was divorced with a teenage son.

A perfect opportunity for this affair presented itself when my father pushed my mother down the stairs of our home and broke her leg. My mom unknowingly healed in bed while her supposed best friend came over to attend to her needs. She appeared to be a loyal friend, cooking her dinner, bringing her magazines, laughing with her, etc. However, afterward, Sally would get in her minivan, pull out of our driveway, park down the street, and then silently sneak back into our finished basement to meet up with my father and satisfy *his* needs.

I assumed this affair would end like all the others. It was always the same: my mother found out, there was a big fight, my parents made up, sometimes my father asked my mother to call the other woman and end the affair, they got along for a while, and then another woman entered the scene yet again. An endless revolving door of women. My mother never stood up for herself and left, so I assumed this wouldn't be any different from all the other times. But it was.

My parents' fighting had become more violent, and eventually I decided to stay home from school. I was worried that one or both of them might kill each other. Skipping classes didn't matter much to me because I had attended so many different schools and had no emotional attachment. I did not have friends to notice my absence or ask where I was. I was invisible, a ghost, so it seemed. The weird chunky girl with the afro who wasn't in class much. When they did see me, I was a target for ridicule. They threw sticky wads of pink gum at me that stuck in my hair. They'd call me names like Porky Pig or pick up their lunch trays and walk away when I sat down at the table where they were. They slid nasty notes in my locker and howled with laughter like a pack of hyenas on the hunt when they brought me to tears. Staying home from school to referee my parents' volatile fights seemed to be a much better option in comparison.

I had often thought of Diane throughout my teenage years— the promised bunny and the softness of her silk blouse brushing across my cheek. I contemplated the many women my father blatantly flaunted—almost daring my mother to leave him or perhaps pleading because he was not strong enough and needed my mother to end the marriage to free us all. I also thought of my mother's desire to keep the family together because that was her top priority. Until my dad pushed her too far with Sally. My mother had crossed a threshold of pain, and she was ready to stand up for herself. If only my mother had had the strength to leave my father years ago, life may have been better for all of us.

CHAPTER 7

A Change of Plans

———————◆———————

My parents told me they were separating after my mom found out about the affair with Sally. This was her breaking point after nearly two decades of enduring the abuse and mistreatment from my father. She finally decided to leave. She was determined, and all her energy was spent deciding what to do next and how she would rebuild her life. I didn't understand many things about what we had to do to make this move possible. In hindsight, I understood her need to pull together her emotional, physical, and financial resources to make it work, but as a teenager who was already beaten down, I felt I needed to make changes that looked a little different from the ones Mom planned to make.

By the end of my junior year of high school, it was clear I would not graduate. I would not attend senior prom, spending hours picking the perfect dress or ordering my cap and gown triumphantly or walking to the podium with my cap tassel swaying with each step and then tossing the cap high in the air as the class of '92 whooped and hollered with excitement for the future. I had lost interest in attending school some time ago because daily survival seemed more important than a piece of paper. All that school had taught me thus far was to dislike the popular cliques and social events and to hide from the never-ending ridicule aimed toward me. Those were valuable lessons I would carry with me for years until I learned differently.

I recognized that my life was out of control. I was choking on my existence for all these reasons: the fighting, my drinking, my involvement with older men, and the lack of direction I had for my future. As I reflected on the many events that I had endured leading up to my parents' official breakup, I determined that the way out was to leave the only place I knew as home. But that still didn't seem like the best solution. Had I ever even known what a home truly was? I didn't even remember all the places I'd lived; they were merely glimpses through the eyes of whoever I needed to be to survive at that point in time. I was unconsciously gliding from one day to another, compartmentalizing my feelings, and looking for the love I so desperately craved in toxic ways, much like my mother had done for years with my father. So maybe I wasn't looking to leave home, because I didn't *have* a home. Maybe I was looking to *find* a home and leave behind the people who made it impossible for that to happen. Though I loved my parents, I knew I could not continue the life that we had made together.

The pine needles cushioned the grassy spot as I sat cross-legged on an area slightly damp from the morning dew. I squinted at the folded, damp, faded paper map of North America I had found walking on the soggy trail at Kennesaw Mountain. Cool crisp mornings were my favorite time to walk and gather my thoughts. Birds chirped and the branches rustled as unseen creatures scurried about. The rest of the world was not yet awake, and the stillness quieted my mind.

The Georgia sunshine warmed my face as I closed my eyes and randomly placed my finger on the map. When I opened my eyes to see where my chipped black-tipped fingernail rested, it rested on a spot right in the middle of Lake Erie. I had a choice to either travel to Canada or Ohio. My eyes settled on Cleveland and I decided this would be my new home.

CHAPTER 8

Home Sweet Home

———————◆———————

When my family lived in an apartment in a suburb east of Atlanta, I met Carrie; she was one of the few classmates I remember after living in so many different places and cities. We were both eleven and loved the five-member new wave English band Duran Duran. We sang for hours, pretending we were famous back-up singers. Shortly after meeting her, she moved to Wooster, Ohio, a small town sixty miles southwest of Cleveland, where she lived with her dad after her mom remarried. One day, when we were both in school together, we decided to exchange phone numbers during lunch in a flimsy sixth-grade yearbook back cover.

"This is my dad's number in Ohio. Call me every day." We pinky-promised that we would keep in touch.

I read her scrawled message in the back of the yearbook that said "Best Friends Forever" in bubble writing. It was one of four short personalized messages displayed in the yearbook, a reminder of the short time I attended that school. The school barely left an imprint. The details were insignificant as I never stayed at one location long enough for school to feel familiar. I read the other messages. "You're the best, Love Tina." "Keep it real, Britney xo." "You're cool, Jenna." I could not recall any of those people. They were strangers. But that didn't matter. The only name that mattered at that moment was Carrie. She would be the key to this next move I was planning to make.

Although Carrie and I never spoke after she left, I decided to try giving her a call. I punched her faded numbers on a pay phone outside a Kroger grocery store in Marietta, a sprawling suburb of Atlanta. Although I thought it was pretty unlikely she could still be reached after all these years, I held my breath as the phone rang. Guilt tugged at my stomach when I thought of the broken promise we had made in the lunchroom ages ago.

As the phone was ringing, my mind traveled down memory lane and the cafeteria smell of pizza and french fries. My thoughts were interrupted when someone answered the phone, a girl who sounded much like Carrie. The voice on the other end confirmed that yes, she was Carrie, and my shock turned into excitement.

What great luck! We spent an hour on the phone catching up on the details of our lives. I quickly learned that our life stories had many unfortunate similarities. She had been living in a trailer with her father, who was an alcoholic, and she was ready for a change. The excitement of having a best friend again now gave me a glimmer of hope about my future. We had several more conversations and made arrangements to live together in Cleveland.

I had never been to Ohio and was excited to go but also sad to leave my mom. The home my parents purchased and promised would be our final home was now in foreclosure. My mother had used all her inheritance from her parents as a down payment at the insistence of my father. When my father decided to move in with Sally, he stopped paying his share of the mortgage and finances, and my mother was ultimately left with no other choice but to let the mortgage payments lapse.

My mom told me she was going to start a new life, too, but she did not know where or how. She knew she could not stay in Atlanta. Perhaps she would move back with her family to Indianapolis or relocate to San Francisco. She had always loved the Bay Area when she was younger and had lived there for a brief time with my older brother Lee when he was a toddler. The future was uncertain for both of us.

A week after the phone call with Carrie, I bought a ticket on Greyhound Bus Lines and packed what I could, stuffing most of it into the small cargo compartment of the bus. My new life began as the bus pulled out of the terminal and headed north.

Carrie arrived a week later. We signed a six-month lease for an inexpensive small single-bedroom apartment that sat over an Italian restaurant in Ohio City. It was a block away from the Westside market and two miles from downtown Cleveland, a perfect location with a bus stop on the corner. I agreed to sleep in the living room because the awning windows overlooked the busy street and I enjoyed watching the people walk by.

As I would lie on the couch, I'd make up stories about the people I saw: who they were and what their lives were like as they hurried down the street, zigzagging and dodging traffic. As I daydreamed, the delicious smell of pasta, garlic and tomato sauce filled the air from the restaurant downstairs.

Shortly after we settled, Carrie and I began to interview at several restaurants in a trendy location called the Flats. I seemed to have trouble getting hired, but Carrie secured a position as a hostess quickly. She worked double shifts and came home early in the morning. Since I couldn't find anything permanent, I lived off odd jobs working at a temp agency.

While living in the apartment in Ohio City, I attempted to enroll in a local community college but was told I needed my GED. *What was a GED?* I wasn't familiar with exactly what that meant. In 1992, the internet was not as accessible, so I researched for hours. I visited the library and learned that it was a Graduate

Equivalency Degree, a diploma for those who did not pursue the route of traditional high school. After many phone calls, I found a location where I could enroll that was accessible from the bus route from my apartment. I signed up for night classes at Max Hayes High School on the west side of Cleveland. I earned my GED one month after my class of 1992 graduated in Georgia. My celebration consisted of a bus ride back to my apartment, watching a Ford plant worker drool on the day's edition of the *Plain Dealer*. He snored loudly, so I adjusted the volume on my Walkman as I listened to the latest CD by Sir Mix a Lot. Little did I know that this seemingly small accomplishment would make it easier for me to step into some opportunities in the future that would change my life.

Carrie started having many male visitors that she entertained in her room during the day. It did not take long to figure out that she was supplementing her income with prostitution. As I watched how she maintained her lifestyle and continued to work at her other job, I briefly considered prostitution myself. Because of my sexual experience during my teen years, I had adopted the mindset that sex was just sex, and if I could make more money in an afternoon than I did in a week of working odd jobs, maybe it was worth it. Thankfully, the Westside market, a block away, had affordable local food vendors, which allowed me to eat for less than twenty-five dollars a week, because with my income, I couldn't afford much more.

As Carrie became more successful in her career, she disclosed to me that she was making hundreds of dollars a day, and she found her customers in the Flats at her hostess job. When I shared with her my interest in what she was doing, she said she had so much work that she would be happy to share her clients. I continued to contemplate this for several days, but something held me back from committing to this lifestyle. Perhaps it was the fear of getting hurt, or maybe I was trying to salvage the tiny bit of dignity I had that I didn't want to lose. Whatever it was, something would not allow me to sell my body.

One day, I sat on a wooden splintered stool in my apartment near the open window, cooling off due to our lack of air conditioning. Below me, two men exchanged money and a small bag next to a blue Ford Taurus. A hooded figure hurried around the corner, and the back window of the car exploded as gunshots echoed in the street. The man standing by the car rushed at the man with the gun, and they struggled as shattered glass crunched beneath their feet. I snapped out of my trance and slammed my body flat on the floor and prayed they did not see me. As I lay there with my heart in my throat, I recalled the many times my father had pulled out his gun on unknown people or during my parents fights when a gun would appear in my father's hand. In those moments, fear and excitement had taken over. But this time, I had no closet to escape to, so I flattened myself on the wooden floor and mentally drifted to a reality of my choice.

It was time to leave; I sensed it. Change was a must. I did not want to be a prostitute or be a part of drama. The relocation to Cleveland was a new start. But I didn't sign up for fighting, shooting, and living with a woman who sold her body while disgusting men with their leering eyes frequented my home. I had not envisioned this. What I tried to escape seemed to follow me from Atlanta to Cleveland. I was now surrounded by a dismal black cloud that unleashed a torrential flood of pain, a flood that I'd silenced for many years.

CHAPTER 9

Reliving the Past

————————◆————————

After earning my GED, I moved into a small one-bedroom apartment in Lakewood, a nearby city, and started a job cleaning stalls in the Cleveland Metroparks, an extensive network of parklands in Ohio. The stables were five miles away, and I could ride my bicycle to work and not have to rely on public transportation. My shift was from four o'clock in the morning until ten o'clock and consisted of feeding the horses, shoveling horse manure, and replenishing their hay. I earned $4.25 an hour, which was minimum wage at that time. Despite the physical level of work I had to do, I loved this job; it allowed my mind to rest and kept my body strong and lean. I never felt lonely around the large majestic horses. I petted their coarse hair as I spent countless mornings looking into their eyes while I shared with them my hopes and dreams for a happier life.

With my GED in hand, I was eligible to enroll in an Emergency Medical Technician (EMT) course at the local community college near downtown Cleveland. The timing worked out perfectly because my mother moved to Cleveland when the bank took possession of the house in Georgia. She said she wanted a fresh start and lived with me in the apartment. She began bartending at a local pub to help pay the rent while I went to community college.

I wanted an exciting job that paid a living wage. During my EMT training, the instructor and I hit it off really well and started a relationship a short time later. Owen was a paramedic in the city of Cleveland. We would frequently hang out at The Dog House after class for pizza, beer, dancing, laughing, and flirting with classmates. Owen had a lot of charisma, direction, success, and confidence—all the things I lacked. The attraction had been instant, but we hesitated and lacked the opportunity to take it further. One night, two weeks after class started, he drove me home. We began a torrid sexual relationship like I'd never experienced before. I quickly became attached to him. He would stop by my apartment when my mom was working and bring me lunch, which we ate in bed between bouts of intense sex sessions. He never stayed past four o'clock in the afternoon, stating he had to go to work, class, or the gym. It was convenient for him to come to my place to see me because I did not have a car and never asked to visit him.

Life was going so well, and I was finally in a relationship with great potential. One day, as I was studying, I was interrupted by a knock. I flung open the door of my apartment, failing to look through the peephole and expecting a surprise visit from my boyfriend. Instead, a blonde curly-haired woman with a very irritated expression stood in front of me. She introduced herself as Heather. Owen's wife.

"Is this a joke?" I asked, wondering how she knew where I lived.

As if she had read my mind, she withdrew a torn edge of college-ruled notebook paper from her purse with my address and phone number on it. She had gone through her husband's—my boyfriend's—wallet and found the paper tucked behind the photo of their two young sons, Jeremy and Nick. They were yet another component I knew nothing about.

She insisted we drive together to confront Owen. Unsure of what to do and quite dismayed by the new information, I agreed. When we walked into his home, Owen was watching a Cleveland Browns football game. The moment he saw the two of us come through the door, his jaw dropped. Heather and Owen both sat down in the living room, Owen opting to stay seated on the black leather couch and Heather in an oversized plaid fabric chair. Their two young toddlers slept peacefully in another room.

I stood by the door, a clear sign in retrospect that I should have taken the escape route when I had the opportunity.

"Me or her?" That was all I remember hearing Heather say as she directly asked Owen what he wanted. I admired her ability to not attack him physically. I'm not sure if I could have kept it together the way she did.

"Heather, I want a divorce," he bluntly answered. In the background, the football announcer excitedly described the play-by-play of the game that was still on the television screen, the volume deafening.

At that moment, I was confronted with the realization that I was now the "other woman" and Heather represented my mother. So many times before, I had imagined what it must have felt like to be in a position like this, and now I knew.

Heather went to the bedroom, woke up her two young boys, and strode out of the front door of the house. I was still standing near the doorway as the remnant of her vanilla perfume wafted by. I watched the event unfold in confusion and then her car peeled out of the driveway. I looked back at Owen.

"Look at that. *Now* we can start our new life," he said, smiling.

I silenced the voice inside my head that warned, "*Run*"

SECTION TWO
A CHANGE OF PLANS

CHAPTER 10

Growing Up Fast

———————◆———————

C ramps and a constant pain near my left hip prompted
a visit to the emergency room in February. A blood test
and ultrasound confirmed an unplanned pregnancy. Disbelief
overwhelmed me. The expression "The apple doesn't fall too far
from the tree," came to mind as I recalled that my mother had
become pregnant at seventeen. I briefly considered an abortion,
but Owen protested and said he would never forgive me because
it went against his religious beliefs. Although I didn't share his
beliefs, I agreed with his decision just like the night Heather
scooped up her children in their pajamas and walked out the
door when Owen chose me.

We left the hospital and drove home. The only sound was the windshield-wiper swoosh as a light rain fell. Owen dropped me off at home and without a word pulled out of the driveway to work. After his car turned the corner out of sight, I shuffled to the front door. Once inside, I went to the flimsy pressed-wood bookshelf, stepped onto the plastic stool, and pulled out my worn copy of *Peter Rabbit* with the cracked spine. My hands, still wet from the rain, stuck to the pages. Flipping to the back page, I stared at the National Guard brochure the recruiter had given me the previous week during a secret stop after the grocery store. I had envisioned joining the National Guard as a paramedic. The military would have offered structure, financial stability, and an escape. I took the brochure, walked to the gas stove, and turned on the knob. As the blue flame flickered, I lit the edge of the brochure on fire and watched my future go up in flames.

The divorce, the transition to being a stepmother, and preparation for motherhood occupied much of my time. I soon quit my job at the stables and moved in with Owen. I was unemployed and pregnant, which qualified me for public assistance, including medical care, food stamps, and a special supplemental program called Women, Infants, and Children (WIC). I had never been on any form of government help and felt ashamed, sheepishly handing my food stamps and WIC coupons to the cashier at the grocery store. I felt as if the other customers in line were staring at me in judgment as I stood there, waiting for the transaction to be completed.

The months went by in a blur, peppered with doctors' visits at a reduced-cost women's medical clinic next to the county hospital. I waited hours in a room filled with other women close to my age. *What were their stories? Had they gotten involved with a married man? Did they question their paths? Did they still cling to their dreams, or had they given them up?* When I asked myself the last question, I realized I had just one dream: to be better than my parents. But already I was repeating their patterns.

While pregnant, I also worked at an ambulance company for a short time until I could not handle the emotional swings any longer. Witnessing young children being mistreated by their parents was heartbreaking. I often saw toddlers playing in a yard or on a porch at two o'clock in the morning without an adult in sight as we drove past homes, responding to an emergency 911 call. We worked on the bad side of town and responded to many calls where parents clearly abused their children. But not much could be done. At times, we weren't called to an accident scene or to assist with an actual medical emergency but were instead called after a death. The ambulance company I worked for had a contract with local funeral homes and when someone passed away in a facility or residence, it was our job to transport the body. The smell of bodily fluids was so strong that I wore Vicks VapoRub underneath my nostrils to avoid contributing more bodily fluids by vomiting while transporting the deceased.

Eventually, when it became too difficult to lift patients onto the stretcher due to pregnancy, I resigned and started working at

Taco Bell. Bean burritos and nachos with cheese sauce provided comfort when I thought about the situation I had placed myself in with Owen. I gained a tremendous amount of weight quickly. I quit after a month and sought employment at a temporary agency. I was promptly placed at the McDonald's headquarters as a receptionist for the franchise owners and office personnel. The position paid a little more than minimum wage and came with normal business hours. The other employees were supportive and always brought me food, contributing to the ninety-pound total weight gain during my pregnancy. My relationship with Owen drastically changed. My role in the household was defined by Owen, and if I did not adhere to his standards, he withdrew his love and berated me. It was best if I behaved the way he wanted.

Owen and I were not married because he was separated and not officially divorced. The divorce was nasty and dragged on for months. Each person was doing what they could to get the upper hand. It was exhausting, but I played along. The drama was familiar, and it was easy to be swept up in the momentum of game playing. Owen often belittled Heather to the children and insisted his child support payments were being wasted on frivolous things, a complaint that would become all too familiar down the road.

Our son, Nathan, was born in the late fall. The birth was painful, yet Owen was insistent on videotaping it so that future EMS classes in the field could use it as a tool. I reluctantly agreed. I had been promised my face would be edited out, but unfortunately that did not happen. For years to come, many people I met who knew Owen also knew exactly what my vagina looked like. Viewers watched a full forty-five-minute video exposing some of my most intimate parts. I learned to accept the embarrassment. Owen just laughed it off.

Since I was on maternity leave, my receptionist position was filled by another employee at the temp agency. Owen insisted I needed to pull my weight in the relationship, and he never failed to mention that it was a lot of weight, referring to my pregnancy weight gain. A month after giving birth, I was starving myself in order to shed the extra pounds. Luckily, at nineteen years old, the baby weight fell off quickly with caloric restrictions and intense exercise. I delayed going to work because I did not want to leave Nathan in daycare with a stranger and the cost of doing so would be more than what I could make working.

Despite my apprehension, six months after our son was born, Owen's divorce was finalized, and we got married. It was a simple affair at the county courthouse with my mom and a witness in attendance. I felt that creating a union officially was the right thing to do because I did not want my son to be raised by unmarried parents. I did what I thought was best, even though it was against my better judgment. Life was about to get interesting very quickly. I had no idea what I was in for.

CHAPTER 11

I Should Have Seen It Coming

---◆---

The abuse started not long after we married. The first sign was when Nathan cried in the middle of the night and Owen would "gently nudge" me, as he described it. It was meant to wake me up so that I could care for the baby, even though I was exhausted and we had previously agreed to rotate nights. The nudge was really a solid kick in the lower back, which often resulted in me hitting my head on the oak wood of the nightstand and landing face down on the carpet. This happened so often that I removed the nightstand from the side of the bed to prevent injury.

My days blurred due to sleep deprivation and anxiety. I took care of Nathan, chasing after him with paper towels and Windex to keep the house spotless. It was my duty to have a clean house and dinner ready for Owen when he came home since I was not working. He often used a white glove to test my cleaning skills.

Owen suggested I get breast implants because my breasts were no longer perky. This was not a surprise because I gained and lost a significant amount of weight from the pregnancy and breastfeeding Nathan. We did not have the money for something so frivolous, so he insisted on taking out a loan at the local credit union to pay for the surgery. Between the child support he was paying and my unsuccessful attempts at finding employment we were barely paying our monthly bills, but I conceded.

After the unpleasant procedure and painful recovery, Owen brought up an idea he had never mentioned before. He wanted me to be a stripper. My resistance to taking off my clothes for money fell on deaf ears. He told me he had done research by spending many hours at various strip clubs talking to the girls to see if it was worth it. As he tried to sell me on my new career path, I realized that he had lied to me. He told me that he had been working late at night, but he had been at strip clubs instead, spending money we did not have to fund his so-called research. I was exhausted, taking care of the baby, and stressed about our finances.

"They make a thousand dollars or more a night!" he exclaimed. "That's more than I bring home in a week! This will not raise the child support for the boys. It's money for us because it's under the table—no taxes and no paper trail."

"Besides, you let me videotape Nathan's birth. Everyone has seen that video. This is just your tits. What's the big deal?" he goaded me, as we ate stew Owen had a special occasion—a celebratory dinner for the new life we would have. I decided I clearly had no say in the matter. Nausea accompanied each bite as he excitedly spoke of the future.

The idea of being a stripper mortified me along with his inconsiderate approach, but his argument held some logic. Hadn't I already crossed some kind of boundary by allowing the videotaping of the birth? I didn't forbid him to show it even though it made me uncomfortable and embarrassed, so maybe he just assumed I was okay with displaying my body.

After I washed the dishes and lined them up perfectly in the cabinet, I opened the pantry door to take out the trash. A fluffy light-brown tail hung out of the bag. I hesitantly moved aside the plastic and saw the tiny carcass of a squirrel. Bile rose in my throat as comprehension set in. He had made the stew with squirrel meat. *Why?* When confronted, he just laughed and told me that it was survival of the fittest. He had shot the rodent in the park with a BB gun, and I shivered as I remembered JP shooting me as I walked home from school.

"If you can't protect yourself, you die. That is just the way life is, and that's how a hunter thinks. Everything weak is prey." His chilling words would forever stay with me.

Two weeks later, I attended amateur night at the Midnight Palace Gentlemen's Club in downtown Cleveland. Amateur night was exactly what it implied. Women took the stage with a fake name as the DJ pumped up the crowd for the new dancers. As Brooke, I untied the thin string holding my red sequined top on, and with one flick of the wrist, my top fell down, exposing my still healing large D breasts. I had covered the angry red incision marks with a makeup concealer.

Flinging the top into the crowd the way I had seen someone do on TV, I attempted to channel my inner vixen and be someone else. Brooke had a confident personality. I slithered around the slippery brass pole, looking sexy in stiletto heels and my borrowed outfit. A balding man standing near the stage made a clumsy effort to put a dollar in my garter belt. His finger lingered longer than necessary on my thigh, which only increased the creep factor. This dance on the stage began a journey I had not planned.

Months into dancing, we were rolling through the money, forcing me to dance more often to cover the expenses Owen was incurring. He became violent and jealous and often locked Nathan and me in the damp chilly basement with small glass block windows for hours when he left for work. As an added measure of horror, he also took the spare car key, so if we found a way out of the basement, we could not leave. We spent the hours watching *Teletubbies* and reading books. With the click of the deadbolt, I escaped into the fantasy land I used to create in the closets growing up, but this time I was locked in a basement with another person to protect.

One day, as the rain splashed against the glass block windows, I stood underneath the rickety wooden basement stairs. I had had enough, and something inside me snapped. I found a Phillips head screwdriver and my hand tightened around the cold plastic handle, preparing to strike. Owen's footsteps grew heavier the closer he came, the creaking on the floorboards getting louder. The jiggling of the door handle as he unlocked it woke up Nathan. My son's sleepy brown eyes locked on mine, and at that moment, I dropped the screwdriver and kicked it away. I did not want to kill his father while my son was watching me, but I knew I had to escape the imminent danger by any means necessary.

CHAPTER 12

Fight or Flight

———————◆———————

The first time I hit Owen back, he was stunned. He responded with a blow to the side of my head with his fist, stars bursting and blurring my vision. The fights were fierce, often landing me in the emergency room. My physical strength was no match for his, and I rationalized away the violence, thinking it was my fault. I'd witnessed my parents fight for so long that it seemed natural to me.

I endured endless visits to emergency rooms, and police were often dispatched to the house. However, police reports were seldom filed. A local investigative journalist contacted me for an interview as part of a feature about safety workers and domestic violence. Where he got my name, I did not know or care but hoped this could somehow give me courage or the resources to escape this prison that was supposed to be home. I recounted to the journalist the denial, the fear, the hopelessness, and the helplessness I felt on a daily basis. He nodded and empathized with me as hot tears streamed down my cheeks. My voice cracked as I tried to portray myself as strong, but I was visibly falling apart. The fear for my son was much greater than the fear for myself. I had told the police the stories after calling 911; they had seen the blood and the bruises, but they never did anything about it. I explained to the journalist that my husband worked for the city and the medical first responders and police knew him. I was usually dismissed by them or told it was somehow my fault or Owen would be quick to file a complaint against me.

In the end, the story did not air, and I assumed political influence was behind the decision. It reminded me of the many times my mother had gone to the police in Georgia asking for help but was dismissed. I could only rely on myself for protection.

I have to get out of here. I can't do this anymore. If I don't leave, he is going to kill us. The fear was no longer about finances; it was about survival. I was worried about protecting Nathan. He was the most important thing to me, and we were going to break free.

After another fight, I found myself bloody and standing outside our single-family house in the snow in my bra and panties. Owen had shoved me and locked me outside after I fought back and threw a small toy ambulance at him. My actions were nothing compared to the blows I had endured. But in retaliation, he pushed me onto the porch in the wintry Cleveland cold.

I stood there shivering while Owen sat inside near the electric heater. Seeing the warm glow made me yearn to be inside, but what triggered a gut reaction was a maternal instinct as I watched my son at the large glass window, waving at me, unaware of the situation. Inside, Owen taunted me, his words coming clearly through the glass.

"Look at Mommy outside. I bet it's chilly out there. What's Mommy going to do? I guess she should learn to act better. Isn't that right, Nathan?"

"Nathan, unlock the door for Mommy," I pleaded through the glass, trying to keep the panic from my voice so that I did not upset him. I was losing feeling in my feet and hands. The crimson blood thickened underneath my nose as it began to freeze.

Realizing I needed to do something quickly, I told my son I loved him through the glass and walked away, flagging down a car. The fear of being attacked by a stranger was less than my fear of freezing to death. I had learned that calling law enforcement did no good from my previous experiences. An elderly man with thick eyeglasses stopped his car, ran to the trunk, and pulled out a wool blanket. He wrapped it around my shoulders, the scratchy material rough against my chilled shivering skin. He drove me to his ranch-style brick home so I could clean up and decide on the next step. He insisted we call the police, but I begged him not to. His wife suggested seeking advice from an attorney they knew. I showered in a bathroom that reminded me of my grandparents' small shower with yellow tiles. Afterward, I slipped into a gray sweatsuit his wife left on top of the counter next to the sink. After I dressed and gathered my thoughts, the couple drove me to the attorney's office, and we began the divorce process.

CHAPTER 13

From Here to There

———————◆———————

Since I had already walked with Owen through a divorce, I knew the tricks he was likely to use—the same tactics he used with Heather—and he did not hold back. He had me arrested at work, weeks after the incident when he locked me outside in the snow. I was charged with domestic violence for assaulting him with the toy ambulance. At the end of my shift, as I exited the stage at the Midnight Palace, two police officers confirmed my identity and handcuffed me in front of the wide-eyed patrons. They guided me into the caged backseat and drove downtown. I was wearing nothing more than my stiletto heels and a black pleather stripper outfit. I spent two days in the tiny jail cell with nothing more than a metal cot and a toilet. Staring at the ceiling unable to sleep, I realized that this man was more than dangerous; he was conniving and ruthless. After I was bailed out, the process dragged on for months with multiple court hearing continuances requested by Owen's attorney. Eventually the charges were dropped due to insufficient evidence and the failure of Owen to show at scheduled proceedings.

The divorce was stressful and costly with emotional warfare that was agonizing. The judge granted me full custody after months of painstaking mediation and parenting classes. The process scarred me emotionally, physically, and financially for years to come. Owen continued to be a threat and hung in the background like a nightmare waiting to turn into a reality, but I continued moving forward and did the best I could for our family of two.

I started working at a different strip club with loose house rules. Strippers, bartenders, and servers made big money at these places. In Ohio, strippers had no-contact rules, but some establishments found ways around this or had connections with the local authorities so that officials would look the other way. They alerted the club owners to any upcoming police vice visits. When authorities arrived, the dancers kept the required legal distance and obeyed the published state laws. Regulars were familiar with the routine and continued to tip well.

With the increase in income from the new club, I moved into a rented condo in a suburb east of Cleveland, and on nights

Nathan was with his father for visitation, I worked. This allowed flexibility to be at home with him and eliminated the need to hire a babysitter. During this time, I found a familiar way to cope. In order to escape a lifetime of fear and pain, I defaulted to using alcohol and often drank when I was dancing. It was easy because part of a stripper's job was to sell overpriced drinks. The girls were motivated to do so because if we did not reach the shift goal, we would have to buy them ourselves.

The more I drank, the more daring I became on stage and the less I remembered. I could forget the leery gaze of the men, the lewd comments they made as they placed money in my garter belt, and the hoots and hollers as my top fell away to the perfectly timed beat of the music I'd picked out with the DJ. Alcohol helped numb the pain so that I could keep working and disengage from my reality.

I generated most of my income and developed a high degree of disdain for men during table dances. A table dance, at a minimum, was twenty dollars per song, often with a tip. If a customer wanted to bypass the dance and talk, the price was set at seventy-five dollars for ten minutes. The customers told me how beautiful I was and shared what they wanted to do to me as they licked their lips. During the dance, they would try to lick my breast as I seductively sawed back and forth with my hand on each of their shoulders for support. Or they would grind their crotch up to meet my backside as I hovered an inch above their lap. They insisted on "getting their money's worth." I disconnected from their actions with the help of strong Long Island Iced Teas and often thought about my grocery list or household chores that needed tending when I returned home.

I missed classier clientele at the Midnight Palace, including the bouncers who paid attention unless told otherwise. I had started my exotic-dance career there and was spoiled by the house moms, women who provided necessities for the dancers, such as deodorant, lipstick, perfume, tampons, etc.

A handful of regulars frequented the Midnight Palace and Love Shack, including Larry. He was my first customer and we had met during a slow afternoon shift at the Shack. I preferred the lunch crowd because the customers did not linger and followed the house rules. Larry worked at Lincoln Electric, a global manufacturer of welding products, and he boasted he was paid well and had money to spare. I could rely on Larry to pay me a minimum of a thousand dollars a week. He was the only customer that did not try to convince me to have sex. Larry enjoyed our conversations, and I appreciated that he valued my mind more than my body.

On Thursday, Larry brought in a handful of flyers from the Midnight Palace advertising a Friday night stripper competition. I grabbed the dozen flyers, tucked them in my garter belt, and took the stage without another thought. After my set, as I walked back to the dressing room, I counted the dollar bills, pushed open the dressing room door, put my money in my locker, and changed for my next stage set. The Midnight Palace flyers snagged as I slid into my leather thong, so I placed them on the mounted table in front of the lighted mirrors. Asia, another dancer, entered through the swinging door and told me I had another regular, Gene, waiting for me. He tipped well, so I hustled and touched up my red lipstick, fluffed up my curls, snapped my garter belt back in place, and rushed out the door.

Two days later, I returned to work. As I got ready for my shift, Carmine, the owner, asked me to come into his office, a wood-paneled chamber with a secret entrance. The only time he asked dancers to enter his office was so that they could sexually pleasure him. I'd never had an encounter with him and did not want to now. I hesitantly walked in. A large assistant who was serving as a bodyguard stood in the far corner and looked me up and down with the same lust in his eyes that the customers had when I went on stage.

"Yes?" I said with obvious uncertainty.

"Do you know why you're here?"

"No," I responded. If it wasn't sex he wanted, I had no idea what this summons could be about.

"Explain this to me." He pulled from the table sitting next to his recliner the Midnight Palace flyers I had left on the dressing room counter.

My mind was blank. *How did he get the flyers? Why is it a big deal?*

Then he clarified, "Asia brought these to me. She ratted you out. You are moonlighting at the Palace and trying to poach my girls."

I stammered to explain but could not get out the words. *That conniving backstabber!* She was always trying to steal my regulars. She was cutthroat and would do anything to eliminate the competition. *Well played, Asia.* She had won this time.

"Clean out your locker and get out of my club. You have two minutes to get the fuck out of here, or I'm blowing off your knee caps!" His choice of words became much more hostile as obscenities and spittle flung from his mouth right toward me.

Carmine began to count in a low voice, "One Mississippi, two Mississippi, three Mississippi," and pulled out a shotgun from the side of the recliner. *Holy crap! I've got to get out of here!* I didn't even stop to clean out my locker. It was winter, and I did not stop to get my snow boots or coat. I just grabbed my purse and stumbled out the back door, the frigid air biting into my bare skin, the high heels crunching on the compacted ice as I struggled to keep my balance. I had such an odd feeling of *déjà vu*, just like when Owen had locked me outside in the bitter cold. Only this time, I was lucky enough to have a car parked out back. The snow was light, so I didn't need to take time to clear off the windshield. I quickly slid behind the steering wheel; the leather seat interior felt as if I were sitting on a block of ice. I clumsily inserted the key into the ignition, started the engine, jammed on the gas pedal, and fishtailed out of the Love Shack driveway back to the safety of my condo to figure out what to do next.

CHAPTER 14

Friends and Foes

———————◆———————

I decided to pass my time doing what I was accused of doing: working at the Midnight Palace. I was new again and could only secure a few shifts a week. That was okay because Crystal, one of the dancers from the Love Shack, had invited me to go to Miami with her and her boyfriend, Dale. She said he had work to do, and she and I would hang out and not to worry because he would give us spending money.

We boarded the flight to Miami International Airport, took a taxi to the infamous Grand Plaza Hotel, and checked into a spacious room with a breathtaking panoramic view of the sparkling

Atlantic Ocean. I had never been in such an upscale room before. I immediately rushed over to the balcony and took in the gorgeous ocean view, not realizing there was only one king-sized bed.

Dale went to work, and Crystal and I relaxed at the spa, ate lunch at the hotel restaurant, and ordered an expensive bottle of red wine, another first for me. After finishing two bottles of the bitter wine, we slipped into our bikinis, sat by the sparkling blue pool, and quenched our thirst with ever-flowing mimosas. The crisp and cool drinks were refreshing in the hot Florida sun.

Dale returned later that evening with a broad smile. He kicked off his snakeskin cowboy boots and unbuttoned his jeans. I went to the bathroom and turned on the sink faucet, splashing my hands in the warm water as if I had a purpose to be there. But I was just trying to kill time and formulate a plan of escape. At some point, I knew I had to open the door, but I delayed as long as I could. When several minutes had passed and I could not stall any longer, I opened the door, and Crystal and Dale were naked in bed, kissing each other. Crystal's roaring tiger tattoo on her lower back glistened with sweat.

"Ummm. Well, you guys, I'll let you do your thing, and I'm going downstairs." I stammered as I looked for a room key so I could make a quick exit.

"What, darling? No, no, no. You come over here with us. The party isn't starting without you. We have a spot right here in the middle of us," Dale said. His words were thickened by whisky.

Oh boy, I thought. *What am I supposed to do now? Crystal didn't say anything about this. I had no idea that sex was part of the deal. How could I have been so naive?*

Of course, Dale wasn't just doing this to be nice; no guy invites a stranger on an all-expenses paid trip without expecting something in return. I also connected the dots and realized that his business was drugs. Crystal had mentioned something about this, but I had chosen not to listen because I was fixated on a fun trip in Miami away from dreary Cleveland.

"I'm on my period." I searched for an explanation that I could also use as an excuse.

"Don't matter, I like it that way," he said.

I could see there was no getting out of this. As I slowly walked to the bed, I located the safe space and retreated into my mind—the same place I had gone so many times before since childhood. I needed to be whoever he wanted so I could survive.

Several hours later, the sun had set, and the room had fallen dark. A soft glow of moonlight provided the only light in the room. I had fallen asleep on the far side of the bed and woke up to something cold and hard pressed against my cheek. My mind did not register what it was as I was foggy from all of the red wine and mimosas combined with the sun and sex.

"Good morning." Dale's gravelly voice was too close to my ear. I opened my eyes wide as he stood over me. His breath was stale with the smell of Marlboro cigarettes and a hint of liquor.

The next sound sent chills up my spine. *Click.* He had cocked the gun. A gun with what I assumed had real bullets in it was now pressed against my face. He jammed it harder into my cheek, pushing against my teeth, the steel metal chilled against my skin.

"You are a whore. Get out of my room before I kill you." *Was I really hearing these same words again?* I flashed back to the echo of a month ago in Carmine's office. What had I done wrong? I had succumbed to his demands the previous night. I thought I did everything right, and now he thought I was a whore. I met his eyes, wild with craze. I knew he meant it.

"Can I get up so I can get my stuff?" I stammered, fearful that the gun was going to discharge. My heart raced in my chest. I thought about Nathan and that he might never see his mom again. I would be just another statistic, and Owen would raise him. That realization scared me more than Dale. Crystal was lying still on the far side of the bed, her back to us. *Was she asleep, or had he killed her?*

"*Go!*" He yanked me up by my hair, throwing me into the wall. He walked over to my inexpensive suitcase with my clothes still in it, picked it up, stepped out onto the balcony, and threw it over the railing from the tenth floor. Next was my rhinestone-covered denim purse, but first he turned it upside down so all of the contents spilled out and then tossed the empty shell of the bag after it.

Then he charged at me and shoved me into the hallway with only a thin white bed sheet covering my sunburned body. With as much humility as I could muster, I took the elevator to the lobby where a police cruiser was in the valet area. I assumed someone had heard the commotion or perhaps seen the suitcase and other contents strewn across the lawn. Some of it had undoubtedly blown much farther, carried away by the ocean breeze.

Immediately my sheet-clad appearance drew the attention of an officer, and I told him those were my belongings. He asked what room I was in, and as I was about to tell him the story, I realized this was like when I was young and needed to keep a secret with Diane and my Uncle Stephen. I was not going to tattle on a drug dealer and put myself in more danger. I had escaped the room alive, but there was no need to make the situation worse. I knew from experience that the police could not be trusted.

"I don't remember. I met a guy and had too much to drink. I went to his room, and he got mad. I can't even remember his name," I lied.

The police officer directed me to sit in the backseat of the police cruiser as he relayed my information over the handheld radio. He was informed by a crackly voice that I did not have outstanding warrants. He offered to gather up my belongings and take me to the station to figure out what to do. He asked why I was in Miami as he wove through traffic on the crowded highway. I lied again and told him I hitchhiked from Cleveland to Miami by myself just for fun. I don't think he believed the story, but he responded with a nod and told me he had a daughter about my age and suggested I should call someone to help me to find a way home.

At the police station I hesitantly called my father in Georgia and asked for money to get home. I knew he could Western Union the funds, but he told me no. He insisted it was my responsibility to clean up this mess and then he hung up. I was heartbroken.

The police officers became resourceful and provided me with a pair of men sweatpants, a Miami Dolphins jersey, flip flops, and enough money to purchase a ticket home. The police officer with the kind eyes gave me a ride downtown and waited with me until the Greyhound Bus Lines depot opened. He firmly told me to be careful and to get my life together.

I boarded the bus, found a seat toward the back, and settled in for the thirty-six hour journey home. The realization a gun had been aimed at me twice within a month sunk in and it scared me. *How had I ended up here? Where was I going in life?* I had to make changes now.

The police officers had gathered up enough money to purchase a bus ticket, but no one, including me, thought about how I would pay for food. At scheduled stops passengers stepped off to use the restroom, stretch their legs, or look at the tacky gifts. I lingered so that I was the only one left on the bus. I rummaged through their bags searching for food. I lived on Pop Tarts, Cheetos, a half-eaten McDonald's hamburger, M&M's, and peanut butter crackers. I drank water from the bathroom faucets. I was always the last to reboard, hoping to avoid suspicion if someone noticed their bag had been tampered with.

I had reached a new low. *When I get back home, things will be different*, I swore to myself.

CHAPTER 15

Climb the Ladder

———————◆———————

The time to exit the adult entertainment industry was approaching quickly. In my heart, I knew I was ready to move on and abandon the sense of false security the money created. Many of the dancers had issues with substance abuse, violence, and other destructive behaviors—all things I was familiar with. I had been walking a tightrope, and it was becoming harder to resist succumbing to the allure of other ways to escape my pain.

The line between my personal and professional life had become blurred and keeping them separate was impossible. At the grocery store with Nathan, I once heard someone call out "Brooke," and

I quickly pushed the rattling cart faster ahead. I had clothes on, no makeup and my blonde curls were hidden underneath an Atlanta Braves baseball cap. *No one could recognize me.* The man came up behind me and pinched my butt; humiliation radiated throughout my body. *I'm nothing more than meat for someone to take a piece of.* The sudden realization was like a foggy day when the sun eventually burns off the clouds and then you can clearly see the landscape. I was prey. I truly believed that this was my future and nothing would change unless I took action now and created a new life. I often imagined attending career day at Nathan's school and speaking to other parents in front of his class with the eager young faces looking at me with anticipation at the exciting job I would share with them. I did not know what that job would be, but it did not include stories of men masturbating in a dark corner while getting a table dance or chasing me down in a grocery store.

After my second near-death experience and return from Miami, I never returned to the Midnight Palace or any other strip club again. I was now a waitress at Hooters! The infamous restaurant chain that targeted men with the allure of wings, beer, sports and beautiful servers. My idea of climbing the ladder was adding a layer of clothing equivalent to a rung at a time. I proudly slid the silky orange short shorts over my slim legs, slipped the snug white tank top on and tied the laces of my white sneakers to start the day. I excitedly made my way to our group meeting where we did a huddle and a cheer before we began each shift.

The atmosphere was upbeat, the lunch crowd mellow, and the girls were like sorority sisters I never had. The restaurant had rare drama: a patron who had a little too much to drink or made an inappropriate comment. Businessmen came in for lunch and left without lingering or behaving poorly. When a sitter was unavailable to watch Nathan, he would come to work with me and shoot basketball hoops by the hostess stand or color in his Power Rangers coloring book in a booth. All the girls and customers alike gushed over him. It felt like the big, loving family I yearned for my entire life. This location felt safe. Until it wasn't.

I worked at Hooters for two years, beginning my career there in the trendy area of Cleveland called the Flats. The restaurant's spacious deck stood on stilts atop the Cuyahoga River at the mouth of the entrance to Lake Erie. In the summer, the sun hit the water, and a million prisms sparkled, making the lake look as if it were made of diamonds. The manager's brother, Ron, rented jet skis on the corner of the patio. All day long, the roar of boats, large and small, blended in with the Jimmy Buffet soundtrack playing over the speakers. The delicious aroma of fry oil and chicken wings hung in the air.

The money was not great during the day, but I was willing to make less money in exchange for the laidback clientele. Occasionally, I worked the night shift to make more money or fill in for other girls. Each time I worked the night shift, I did not exercise the willpower I needed to kick my alcohol habit and easily slipped back into destructive drinking habits. A late-night shift often ended in the hot tub with unlimited alcohol provided by the shift manager and other workers from clubs down the strip who attended the after-work party.

One morning, I woke up early on the floor of an unfamiliar apartment. I could not remember what had happened except I had gone to the bathroom to change my clothes. Everything else was blank. John, the cook, told me Allison, his girlfriend, had found me naked on the employee bathroom floor. They tried to get me to wake up and debated taking me to the hospital. They decided to get me dressed and take me home with them. Unfortunately, they lived on the fifth floor with no elevator, so they dragged me up the stairs, leaving my back bruised and sore.

I still have no recollection of what happened that night. My best guess is that someone put a date rape drug in my bottle of Corona. The assault more than likely had occurred in the small bathroom of the restaurant.

I left their apartment feeling deflated and empty. The next day, bruises resembling fingers and handprints showed up on my inner thigh, unlikely the result of John and Alison moving me up the stairs. I had no idea what had transpired. Perhaps it was best that way. For all I knew, John and Allison had assaulted me. The terrifying feeling of not knowing who to trust intensified. I thought I would be safer at Hooters and had inadvertently set a trap for myself by becoming careless and letting down my guard.

CHAPTER 16

Wings and New Things

———————◆———————

There was a management change at Hooters shortly after the bathroom incident. The new manager, Seth, had a negative attitude and addressed women in a condescending way. It reminded me of how the managers at the strip club treated the dancers. At the end of a slow afternoon shift, I was counting out tips in the office. Seth snuck behind me and grabbed my hips, his pelvis thrust against me. I froze, uncertain of what to do. So many times before, I had retreated back into my head and let my body endure a separate reality, hoping it would not resurface in my subconscious. As women, we are taught to protect ourselves, but sometimes we cannot—no matter our best efforts—and so we shut down instead. The psychology behind it can be complicated and confusing. Your brain is saying *fight back*, but your physical body is paralyzed. I mentally identified as a victim.

Emily, the day bartender, walked into the office, and Seth jumped away from me as I stammered out an incoherent sentence in an attempt to camouflage my humiliation. He sat at his desk, no doubt to hide the erection that moments ago had been pressed against me. I walked out of Hooters with tears in my eyes and decided to never return.

The next week, I climbed another rung of the ladder by adding more clothing and started bartending at a popular sports bar franchise and dining restaurant, Buffalo Wild Wings (BW3). This time, I wore a polo shirt, long khaki pants, and the same white sneakers. I worked with four other bartenders, and we hustled to make shared tips. We didn't have any time to chat with customers because BW3 was busy. We always had something to do and I did not have to be concerned with how sexy I looked to make money.

I began to feel that I needed to find a dad for Nathan—a reliable man with a regular job and without a lot of drama. I was tired of sending Nathan to different babysitters. When my mom moved to Cleveland after divorcing my father to restart her life, she helped out as much as she could. But she worked long hours to support herself, so she was not always available. Nathan needed a stable father figure.

And then I met Jeff. I was working the expedited drink walkup line that night during a televised Indians baseball game, and when he ordered a beer, he winked at me, clearly interested. He was cute, but I was not instantly attracted to him. Even so, I let my guard down at the sight of his short brown military haircut, warm chestnut colored eyes, and casual friendly demeanor. I talked with him during my break and we agreed to meet up the following Friday.

We spent weekends at my apartment with Nathan playing board games and watching Disney movies. The conversations were superficial and shallow, and we did not have much in common. But Nathan loved him and was genuinely happy. Jeff also provided an added layer of protection from Owen because, with a man in my life, I did not feel like a target.

Six months passed, and we became engaged in Las Vegas. I called my mom from the lobby of the Luxor casino to tell her. A long pause was followed by a sigh heard over the whirling slot machines; her disapproval was apparent. She could not understand my rush to get married, but I knew why. I was anxious to secure my future so that Nathan and I were not left exposed.

CHAPTER 17

Second Chance at Love

————————— ◆ —————————

Three months later, we were married in a small quaint ceremony in front of forty friends and family members by a small lake on an unseasonably hot September day. As I marched down the aisle to violinists playing Pachelbel's Canon in D, I knew I was getting married for all the wrong reasons. That same uneasiness still overwhelms me every time I hear the melody.

We honeymooned in the Caribbean on a week-long cruise with Nathan. We agreed not to use birth control, and I became pregnant. I continued to bartend up until a week before Gabriella was born, but I became increasingly more uncomfortable each day due to the long hours spent on my swollen feet and an achy back. I couldn't resist a continuous supply of cheese fries from the kitchen staff, which contributed to another enormous weight gain.

Married life was mundane during this time because, once I entered the third trimester, I was too exhausted to do more than work and care for Nathan, who was six years old. He was excited to meet his new sibling. Gabriella was born in the summer and the family felt complete. It was time to focus on my education.

I enrolled in business classes online at Tri-C, a local community college. These were time-consuming because online internet courses were new and not as efficient and effective as they are now. I became discouraged and eventually resigned myself to the fact that my life was to bartend, be the best mother possible for Gabriella and Nathan, and deal with a mediocre marriage with little intimacy.

I drank my morning cup of coffee and scoured the latest edition of the Entertainment Book, a local coupon book sold to members of the community with discounted events, goods, and so forth, for a weekend family activity. I glanced down at a coupon for a thirty-minute introductory flight in a small four-seat airplane at the local airport located between downtown Cleveland and Lake Erie. For some reason, this activity caught my attention even though I had a terrible fear of flying, and I tore out the coupon.

The thought of an airplane instantly evoked panic. I had never had a bad experience and had only been in an airplane a few times. But I needed medication each time I flew to reduce my anxiety. I maximized the effects by washing down the pills with a shot of vodka at the airport bar on the way to the gate. I could not compartmentalize flying as a passenger like I did when I was in danger or when a nonconsensual event was occurring. I was even more apprehensive about flying after the horrific acts of 9/11 one year earlier.

As I contemplated all the reasons this wasn't a good idea, a small gentle voice inside my head whispered among all the other chatter and said, "Why not? Just try it." With that, I summoned the courage.

It was a bright, windy morning. I had dropped Nathan off at school and Gabby at my mom's. Butterflies were fluttering in my stomach as I traveled to the airport. I filled out the necessary consent forms without reading them. I knew I'd be too stressed if I read everything that could go wrong beyond what I'd already imagined. I quickly scribbled my signature on the required line, spun around, and met my flight instructor. Katherine. *A woman! What? This is amazing*, I thought. Although I expected a man, I began to build a rapport with Katherine. After thorough instructions on emergencies, an explanation of what was expected of me, and a pre-flight check of the airplane, we were all set to go.

I awkwardly put on the headset and sat in the left seat as Katherine taxied toward the runway. Once we lined up on the painted numbers she pushed the throttles forward, the tiny airplane vibrated with power, and we accelerated quickly as we lifted off.

We reached six thousand feet and she instructed me to place my hands on the controls, or the yoke, which is similar to a steering wheel on a car and helps control the direction of the airplane. I later learned that each seat was equipped with a yoke so that either person could fly. After we were established in level flight, Katherine removed her hands and told me I had full control. I wasn't expecting that. I thought I was just going for an airplane ride and did not know I would get to fly. I apprehensively turned left and right as we outlined the shoreline of Lake Erie. *I was doing it!* I was taking control and could steer this airplane in the sky, something I had been previously afraid to do. At that moment, I began to realize that, just like with this plane, I could take control of my life as well. And I planned to do exactly that.

When the lesson ended, I rushed home, excited to tell Jeff about all that I had experienced. I couldn't wait for him to celebrate my accomplishment, and I thought for certain I could get my private pilot's license for recreational use. It was just what I needed to build confidence, expand my mind, and add excitement to my life. I knew the training was expensive, and I had already considered that I could offset the cost with extra bartending shifts.

For once I saw a better future, not only for myself but for all of us. But I didn't expect Jeff's reaction. He dismissed my idea. He said, "A pilot? That's silly. Why would you want to do that? That sounds really hard anyway, and besides, we don't have the money."

The more he told me it was impossible and how ridiculous the idea was, the more determined and committed I became to actually accomplish my goals. I felt as if I were being pushed into a corner with another door being slammed in my face—out of control with someone else making the decisions for my life. I responded in the only way I knew how—violence toward my husband and my children. I had so much pent-up anger within me that I could not control, and I continued to unleash it at the slightest provocation.

Each day, I felt as if I had been playing a character in a stage production as someone I was not, an actress filling a role that everyone thought I should play. I could not do it anymore. I had to ask better questions of myself instead of playing the victim. Instead of asking, "Why me? How could I have made this mistake again? Why am I so stupid?" I started asking more empowering questions, such as "Where do I want to go? Why do I want to do this? How am I going to get there?" I did not know how, but I knew I wanted to be a pilot. I was tired of merely surviving and was ready to start designing my life. I was still working on exactly what it would take to accomplish that but I had taken the first step by making the decision.

Jeff's lack of support contributed to the rapid deterioration of our marriage. I began to focus on my flying and an escape plan and was no longer interested in building or maintaining our relationship. I did not have the emotional capacity or the desire to carry the added weight of someone who was not supportive. It was full steam ahead, and the anchors in my life that were weighing me down were being lifted and left behind.

CHAPTER 18

A Special Surprise

———————————◆———————————

At twenty-eight years old, which was much older than the industry normal, I started taking flight lessons. I picked up additional bartending shifts at BW3 and also took on a part-time job at Burke Lakefront Airport as a front-desk customer service representative on weekends. I worked at the airport's fixed-base operator (FBO) and provided services to the passengers and crew who flew in on corporate, private and chartered aircraft.

My laborious schedule made it easier to disconnect from my marriage. Five days a week, I picked up extra bartending shifts and worked all night, came home, took the children to school, drove to the airport, took a flying lesson, went back home, and slept until it was time to pick the children back up. I'd study at the bar with flashcards during my shift, and patrons and other employees laughed at me, snickering behind my back and sometimes even to my face.

The balance of being a mother, maintaining a home, working two jobs, and being a flight student was difficult to find. Some days, I wanted to quit and struggled to get out of bed. I stared at the ceiling, questioning if I had the energy to keep going. I knew I had to be strong, but my family was falling apart. I was going heavily into debt by paying for flight school with student loans. Although I was exhausted most of the time, I was confident that it would be worth it. The fear of failure scared and motivated me into action. I did not want to reach the end of my life filled with regrets. I was determined to not only reach but exceed my potential.

A year into flight training, I sat at my desk inside the FBO, reading a biography I had purchased the week prior on clearance at the local bookstore. A man who looked familiar appeared in front of me. As he approached, I noticed that he closely resembled the astronaut on the cover of the new book, *John Glenn, A Memoir.* My initial thought was that I was sleep deprived and was hallucinating. Smiling, he said, "Oh, I see you're reading my book." I was stunned! I tried to discreetly peel the ninety-nine-cent red discount sticker off the cover as I stood. *Isn't it an insult to an author when his book is sold for less than a dollar?* I assumed it was.

Senator John Glenn warmly introduced me to his wife, Annie, and we chatted for a while as they waited for their small private airplane to be fueled before they continued on their journey. We spoke for over an hour, and I shared my aviation goals and aspirations with him. He firmly encouraged me to soar, to not let others decide my fate. He told me, "Follow your heart and live with passion. Do not die with regret."

His fuel stop in Cleveland was unexpected and unplanned, yet I truly believe it was especially for me. I've begun to recognize signs the universe sends our way. *Was it a coincidence or a sign?* In either case, I was thankful for that moment as it encouraged me to continue moving forward.

Senator John Glenn's advice helped me remain focused and resourceful as I continued with flight training, accumulated aircraft flight time and built my network. I also found the time and resources to travel to the Bahamas and Arizona to complete phases of flight training I could not do in Cleveland due to the inclement weather. Each challenge strengthened my resolve.

But the biggest challenges were yet to come.

CHAPTER 19

Sudden Course Correction

———————————— ◆ ————————————

Days before Christmas 2006, my father died at fifty-seven. Although he was not the best role model, his death was a wake-up call. This was the second time that anyone close to me had died, and I realized we can often get caught up in the story we tell ourselves and veer off course. The story is the perception of events based on our personal values, fears, and expectations, which may cause us to miss the bigger picture and can either empower or destroy us. I needed to reevaluate and take an honest look at my situation. My dad's behavior taught me many things, including the importance of raising my standards because in life we get what we accept and tolerate.

There was no funeral or celebration-of-life service. Drama continued to surround my father in death as it had in life. He was cremated without the family's consent. It was given by one of his many girlfriends, Sophia, who had been present at the hospital when he died. Afterward, she promptly cleaned out his bank account and the house they shared. Jeff and I visited and stayed with my brother Eric after Sophia gave us permission to access photos and other belongings that had not been sold or discarded. We sorted through photos of a lifetime far removed and foreign from my life now. This unleashed deep and powerful feelings I'd compartmentalized—feelings of neglect, hurt, anguish, betrayal, abuse. I knew I had to make another change, a massive change. I had no more excuses. I was doing the very thing I was fearful of: living a life filled with regret. I remembered my father's life—his hopes and dreams all tossed into seven cardboard boxes on a cold concrete basement floor, an unfulfilled life.

These two events—meeting Senator Glenn and the death of my father—incidents that occurred three years apart, changed the course of my life significantly. Those experiences gave me a new perspective and greater strength propelling me forward. Within five years, I completed my bachelor's degree in Aeronautical Science and earned a master's degree in Aeronautical Science with specializations in Space Operations and Aerospace Safety Systems. In addition, I became certified as a flight instructor and that allowed me to teach others how to fly. During that time, I decided that, as part of my healing, I had to forgive others for what they had said and done to me, and most importantly, I had to forgive myself. So I did.

I decided that I no longer wanted to remain in my unhappy marriage to Jeff. Our relationship had significantly changed, and since my aviation pursuit had exposed me to so much more of life, I knew divorce was the only solution. Both of us had known the end was near for quite a while. The finale came one snowy day in April 2007 after I had received a phone call from a woman stating she was having sex with my husband. Other women had presented me with similar stories of sexual encounters over the years and I could no longer pretend our marriage was salvageable. In a fit of frustration and relief, I opened the front door and began jettisoning his clothing onto the snow-covered lawn. The neighbors outside shoveling their driveway watched in fascination. It was not the most tactful way to end a ten-year marriage, but someone had to take action, and the phone call had been the catalyst that set the end in motion.

I walked away from the marriage with substantial debt, full custody, and a fresh outlook on life. The divorce was swift; less than a month after I filed, we signed the final papers. In hindsight, it may have been a better financial decision to split the debt. But I just wanted us all to begin living our lives without becoming bogged down in court proceedings and the stress associated with a lengthy custody battle like I had experienced with Owen.

During my divorce, I was employed as a first officer for the corporate sector of aviation. The first officer occupies the right seat in the flight deck and assists the captain with duties. The captain and first officer have the same training but typically the first officer has less experience than the captain in the specific make and model of the airplane. I was flying a Citation V, a mid-size private jet that seated between five and eight people, for high-profile clients when the company experienced a fatal plane crash into Lake Erie.

Another airplane in our fleet had taken off from Burke Lakefront Airport in the early January evening, banked a hard right turn and smashed into Lake Erie one-quarter mile off the shoreline. I was stunned. This was the same airport where I had taken my first flight lesson with Katherine. The aircraft was a reposition, also known as a repo flight to Niagara Falls. A reposition flight is common in aviation when an airplane needs to travel from one city to another to pick up passengers. The aircraft is flown to the city where it is needed with one or two pilots, depending on crew requirements for the type of aircraft. The pilot for this reposition flight was a close friend of mine. I had spent hours flying with Tom and had flown his twin-engine Cessna several times to the Bahamas. We had spent countless hours exchanging flying stories at his home next to a local airport. He was killed, but there were no passengers on board. I was devastated and heartbroken to lose a fellow pilot and friend.

A month after the crash, on Valentine's Day, I was terminated from my position. An outsourced human resources woman from Chicago invited me into the owner's office and let me go. She said it was because I was seeking employment elsewhere and the company could no longer afford to pay me. Yes, it was true I was looking for another flying job. That was the normal progression for a pilot with limited experience to build flight hours in an airplane. The pilot gains experience, which was referred to as building time. Once time and experience requirements were met, a first officer is eligible to become a captain.

Another option was to fly larger equipment, resulting in increased compensation at a different company. This cycle was common and repetitive in the aviation industry. But after the accident, the company had stopped utilizing me as a pilot for unexplained reasons. I was making less than thirty thousand dollars a year, and I was on call 24/7, a controlled lifestyle I did not enjoy. For example, I had flown to Atlanta to connect with family members following my father's death. Less than a day after I arrived, my boss called and told me to return to Cleveland immediately because I needed to fly a trip that evening.

"Death is not an acceptable excuse", he told me.

Jobs were scarce, and since the plane crash, I was not flying. As a pilot needing to build flight hours to gain experience to become a captain, I needed to be in the air, and now I did not have a job. Back to the drawing board I went. This was just another temporary setback that would become a setup for something better down the road.

CHAPTER 20

Welcome Aboard

———————— ◆ ————————

I n 2008, the economy was in a recession, and I was heavily in debt from the divorce and student loans. The home I agreed to keep was underwater by more than half, and I had two young children to support. I had been supplementing my income with student loan money and could not sustain our basic expenses with the job loss. The outlook was bleak but I knew I had to stay in the arena and was confident that another opportunity would present itself.

A friend suggested that I apply to the regional airlines. A regional airline is an airline that operates aircraft to provide passenger air service to communities without sufficient demand to attract mainline service. They operate smaller aircraft, and the average seating configuration is fifty to seventy seats. In 2008, the starting pay for a first officer at a regional airline was eighteen thousand dollars. The airline had a base in Cleveland and was contracted by Continental Airlines. This worked out well because the company was local, and I did not have to endure a commute to another city. Many pilots commute to their domicile. This means they request a standby ticket—if there is an empty seat available—and fly to the assigned domicile to start their work day. It's a brutal way to get to work because the pilot is at the mercy of seat availability, weather, mechanical breakdowns, and competes with other pilots for a seat that is determined by a variety of factors. The upside is that the pilot can live anywhere in the world but must find a way to get to work on their own time without pay, which takes creativity and causes a tremendous amount of stress.

Working at the airlines was fantastic for a few months because I was home many days and could spend time with the children. The downfall was the pay. I was an airline pilot, making poverty-level income and on public assistance. I supplemented my meager income by driving for a ride share company.

My airline opened up a new base in Newark Airport in New Jersey six months after I was hired. I was no longer based in Cleveland and began commuting. My scheduled work days increased and I was only home four to six days a month compared to the eighteen days when I was first hired. I often took the children to work with me on available flights to spend time with them or when I did not have a babysitter. My ex-husband threatened on many occasions to take custody of the children because they were home alone for days at a time. Neighbors or my mom checked in on them or watched them, but it was not an ideal situation. I tried to find another job and knew that if I could just hang tight, my circumstances would change sooner or later.

I often slept in the airport terminal, crew rooms or the park because I could not afford a crash pad. A crash pad is for commuting crew members. It is a room, or often just the use of a bed in a room, and many times a hot bed. A hot bed is a term used to describe the use of a bed that is still hot from the heat of the last crew member who slept there on a rotation when the crew member was unable to commute back home for a variety of reasons: schedule, weather, etc.

The wages I made were too low to pay for one residence, much less rent elsewhere, so I found myself changing into sweatpants in the airport bathroom, taking the bus into New York City, and finding a safe spot to sleep on the grass in Central Park when the weather was warm enough. I used my backpack with my pilot uniform as a cushion. I often thought passengers would be horrified to hear how regional pilots made ends meet, squashing the misconception that airline pilots made hundreds of thousands of dollars. This was true, but only when they flew larger aircraft for major airlines or established cargo carriers. The truth about pilot wages began to surface when Colgan Airlines flight #3407 departed Newark Airport en route to Buffalo and crashed, killing all passengers on board, the crew, and a commuting pilot. This brought to light the exhaustion faced by pilots who were underpaid and deficits in training programs. The first officer working that flight supplemented her income as a barista and had commuted in for the trip with limited sleep. This was combined with a lack of training standards and the failure of the captain to meet these. It would take several years for the government to pass new airline regulations and for wages to be increased.

I continued to go to college and began working online toward my master's degree in Aeronautics for two reasons: I loved learning, and I also needed the student loan money. My financial situation improved slightly when I upgraded to captain three years later. A month of intense training at our facility in Seattle molded me into the position, and I took full responsibility for my crew, aircraft, and passengers. Even though I looked like I had made it from the outside, I thought I was a fraud, an imposter. I thought I had just gotten lucky. But here I was, flying next to seasoned professionals: military pilots, engineers, amazing men, and only a handful of women in this male-dominated industry. They all had jaw-dropping résumés and I did not.

Mentally, I couldn't quite shake my past. I felt like a loser: the dropout, the stripper, the Hooters waitress, the welfare mom, the victim, and all the other labels I plastered on myself. I was asking the wrong questions again, and instead of asking better ones, I buried my past, living in fear that someone would find out my secrets, decide that I didn't belong, and take everything away from me even though I had done all the work, passed all the tests, and fairly earned my seat in the flight deck. I was one of fewer than 450 female airline captains worldwide, responsible for the safe transport of over forty thousand passengers annually. I had even been selected as the captain to fly Ivanka Trump, her security detail, and members of her team while her father was President. I was flying multimillion-dollar aircraft, leading my flight crew, serving as a role model, yet I still felt as if I did not measure up and was not good enough.

The inferior feeling of being a female in the aviation industry was isolating at times. Inappropriate jokes in the crew room and sexual innuendos in the flight deck were not uncommon. Not all male pilots exhibited poor behavior, and several of them have become huge supporters of female rights and are like big brothers to us. But I had been asked on many occasions if I got my job by giving great blow jobs. Many female pilots became accustomed to laughing off the crude comments because it was expected of us, but the residual disgust and shame at the blatant harassment were hard to shake. Several female pilots shrugged and used the excuse of "boys will be boys" to explain the behavior. We knew that if we complained, the consequences of being blackballed in the industry were much harder to overcome than a handful of chauvinistic and sexist remarks. We were, after all, intruding on a career intended for men.

Passengers were also active participants in vile comments. A male passenger once peeked around the flight attendant during the boarding process to look at the pilots. When he saw me sitting in the flight deck, he joked, "Oh, there's an empty kitchen somewhere. Good thing you have a man up there to help you figure out how to use all those buttons and switches."

I was even more caught off guard when a random woman asked me an inappropriate question. I was commuting from Cleveland to Newark in uniform as a passenger, when a woman asked me very loudly as we were boarding if I take time off work "during that time of the month" because "we all know how crazy hormones affect us." Over time, I became numb to the questions, comments, and poor behavior, only to realize much later that the same coping skills I used when I was younger were ones I used now when placed in awkward situations.

I had a series of disastrous, drama-filled relationships after my divorce that did not help my confidence and that reinforced the feelings I had always had toward men. The first man I dated after my divorce was a barista who was ten years younger than me. He was better suited as a playmate for my children than as a partner. I also dated an Air Force colonel who cheated; an air traffic controller who was also an alcoholic and a serial cheater; and a womanizing mainline airline captain. I chose to stay with all of them even though I knew it was not healthy. But it was familiar, and I chose to play the victim in my head when they ended it with me. Drama was familiar, and that, combined with cheating, was a common denominator with each of them. I had no boundaries and still had not recognized my true worth. I could have ended any of these relationships at the first sign of dysfunction, but I did not.

CHAPTER 21

Wake-Up Call

———— ◆ ————

After an unexpected skin cancer diagnosis during a routine dermatologist visit, I remembered Senator John Glenn's advice: "Do not die with regrets." I had forgotten these words in the blur of avoiding bankruptcy, the drama of unhealthy relationships, the hectic pace of working on my master's degree, the exhausting life as a single parent, and a demanding career. It was time once again to reevaluate what direction I wanted my life to go. I believe this happens often in life. These slight pivots allow us to make necessary course corrections that we may not otherwise take. Sometimes circumstances reveal the need for a course correction, and if we adjust, we can get back on the path we were intended to be on.

A medical condition can be the death of a pilot's career. Losing my sole source of income was a major concern as a single parent. As pilots, we must maintain what the industry refers to as a medical certificate. This accompanies our pilot's license and is a requirement. Airline pilots require a checkup with an aviation medical examiner every six to twelve months, depending on the age of the pilot. If a medical certificate is lost for a number of reasons, it can be a devastating blow to a pilot because we are unable to work. Flying was my livelihood. Fortunately the diagnosis did not disqualify me from flying after more testing revealed I was cancer-free after areas where it was present were treated. I modified my lifestyle habits and started eating a plant-based diet, committed to exercising more, and worked on reducing stress.

An unexpected blessing was that the skin cancer diagnosis introduced me to my love of running. I had been in the woods near my house when I received the call with the upsetting results from my dermatologist and did not know what else to do, so I just started running to release the stress from my body. After the short run, I felt rejuvenated and knew I needed to incorporate running and being outdoors into my daily routine.

In an effort to reconnect with nature and myself, I frequently escaped into the woods of the Kenai Peninsula in Alaska, using my free travel flight benefits as a pilot to commute to work and back to my home in Cleveland. I'd fly into Anchorage, a small city that looks deceptively quiet but that is full of history and culture. After landing, I would rent a car at the airport and drive the short distance out of the city and then south on AK-1. The highway is bordered by sparkling Cook Inlet, glaciers, thick trees, and towering mountains. The four-hour drive toward Homer on the Kenai Peninsula felt majestic and surreal. I developed a game to see how many moose I could spot during the drive. Several times, I saw bears walking along the edge of the woods or the side of the road on my drive, and each time, I silently prayed I would not break down or get a flat tire.

On one of my first visits, I drove outside of Homer, where I found a small one-hundred-square-foot cabin a mile from the main house owned by an eighty-year-old woman, Nellie. The cabin had been recommended to me by the cook at a local restaurant. I easily found the location and approached a woman chopping wood. When she turned around and we made eye contact, I saw a woman matching the description the cook had given me. I was surprised to see her swinging an axe at eighty years old. Nellie queried me as to why I wanted to rent the cabin and asked if I knew how to protect myself from dangerous men and from the three types of bears—grizzly, brown, and black— commonly seen in the area. Luckily, I had a handgun, which was not adequate protection from wildlife but could deter an aggressive man if necessary. I was grateful for the firearm and self-protection training I had received in the government's Federal Flight Deck Officer Program years earlier.

The log cabin sat on a steep ledge overlooking Kachemak Bay; a steep drop of at least 150 feet was steps away from the entrance.

The deep blue hue of a glacier reflected sunlight through the front of the small cabin with all glass windows. The brilliant light shimmered off the water. The structure had no electricity, no phone and the only source of heat was a wood-burning stove. Nellie agreed to rent the cabin to me for ten dollars a night as long as I promised to use the gun to protect myself.

The first night terrified me as large animals, presumably bears and moose, roamed around the cabin. I lay awake and conjured up scary scenarios: an earthquake shaking my small cabin off its flimsy foundation, sending me plummeting into the bay; a hungry bear bursting through the glass window in search of food; or a felon fleeing from authorities stumbling across my cabin and trying to hide there. I quickly learned that if I was going to enjoy Alaska, I had to stop imagining worst-case scenarios. The safest thing to do was stay indoors at night. The real threats included a walk to the outhouse at night and possibly losing my footing, which could send me tumbling down the cliff, or an encounter with a bear. My simple solution: a large empty glass pickle jar sat next to my bed to pee in and a flashlight.

Despite these challenges, the view was breathtaking, and the price was certainly right. I contemplated moving to Alaska because of the sheer majestic feeling the state embodied.

SECTION THREE
NICARAGUA

CHAPTER 22

Something Old, Something New

———————— ◆ ————————

"Come to Nicaragua," Valerie, a longtime friend and pilot, suggested on the other end of the phone as I plucked weeds from the backyard flower beds at my home in Cleveland. Airplanes were taking off in the background on her end of the call. *She must be at work*, I thought.

"Why? And to be honest with you, I don't even know where Nicaragua is. Plus I don't speak Spanish," I replied. I desperately tried to recall information about this country. I put the phone on speaker and referenced Google to find it on the map. *There it is!* I said to myself as I stared at a small Central American country nestled between Costa Rica and Honduras.

Valerie continued, "My sister and I are going down for a golf-and-surf vacation for three weeks. It will be great and a lot of fun! You have free travel benefits, and you can stay with us. All you need to know is how to ask where the bathroom is. They all speak English there. Plus we are staying at a high-end resort," she reassured me.

I felt adventurous and wanted to embrace life more. So I responded, "Okay, I'll go." I had no idea that my life was about to take a drastic shift.

I prepared for the trip, which would be in less than two weeks. The required vaccinations alarmed me because this was my first experience and the names seemed scary. *Where the heck do I get hepatitis A, hepatitis B, typhoid, yellow fever, rabies, meningitis, polio, measles, mumps, rubella, tetanus, diphtheria, pertussis, chickenpox, shingles, pneumonia, and influenza vaccinations?* The list was extensive, and after many hours of searching through my medical records, I found that many of these had been administered throughout my life. I only needed yellow fever, typhoid, hepatitis B, and flu shots. The frustration of locating a facility that met the requirements almost caused me to cancel the trip. I gave up on the flu shot, but I knew I would definitely need the vaccinations for yellow fever and typhoid fever, or the trip was off. One last call to Walgreens saved the day. *Who would have thought?* I did not meet the recommended time lapse between taking the live dose and my departure date, but I figured it was better than nothing.

I downloaded a Spanish application on my phone to help me recall basic high school Spanish vocabulary. I had visited Cancun years ago with Jeff, and not speaking Spanish had not been a problem at all. I assumed it would be the same in Nicaragua.

I arrived in Managua, the capital, in the middle of July in the late afternoon after a delayed connecting flight in Houston. When I cleared customs at the airport in Nicaragua, I quickly realized I had underestimated the importance of speaking Spanish. Once I exited the airport, at least a dozen taxi drivers were trying to get my business, and I did not understand a word they said except for, "Taxi, lady?" Their aggression was unnerving. My cell phone did not have service, and I slightly panicked. This looked like a tough country, and I had not sufficiently prepared myself. Luckily an English-speaking airline crew was walking toward their hotel shuttle at the curb, and I asked them for help. They directed me across the street to the Best Western but told me to take a cab because it was a dangerous area despite the short walk.

I hailed a taxi and made my way to the hotel. Once I checked in, I connected to the internet and messaged Valerie. She told me I should have traveled the next day as planned because she had arranged for shuttle transportation from the airport. She warned me not to leave the hotel room and advised me she would reschedule the shuttle.

The following day, the shuttle picked me up and drove the two hours to the resort on the Pacific Coast. We passed oxcarts carrying people who were sitting on top of piles of wood or other materials. The large painted buses proudly displayed various religious symbols as passengers hung off the sides through the open windows and the back exit door as they stood on the rear bumper. Cows freely roamed the streets, and we stopped frequently to let a herd pass. The animals looked thin compared to what I saw in the United States. Their ribs and hip bones protruded through their dust-covered hides.

The quaint hotel was upscale but it was not a resort by American standards and the staff spoke broken English. It was two stories high with a small outdoor restaurant and an undersized pool. Brown grass surrounded the area on the golf course, and a surf shop offered lessons.

I spent three exciting days on the shore of the rocky ocean at the resort. Surprises included riding horses on the secluded beach and encountering locals walking pigs on leashes. The guide told us the horses had a tendency to throw the riders, or at least that's what we pieced together between the combination of his limited English and our poor Spanish. He assured us not to worry at the exact moment the horse Valerie rode, named Starbuck, folded his long legs and almost rolled over on her. She quickly jumped out of the way before he crushed her in the sand.

We spent hours drinking the local beer, Toña, and eating *gallo pinto*, a rice-and-red-bean combination that is a staple in Nicaragua and is served with everything. Valerie, Alexis, and I relaxed by the pool often, dipping in to cool ourselves from the unrelenting heat. We chatted about our career successes, love woes, and hopes for the future.

The biggest surprise came at the end of my visit. The hotel staff had arranged a personal driver to take me to the airport. I said my goodbyes to the girls after a leisurely morning walk on the isolated beach, looking for the perfect seashell to bring home as a souvenir.

It was time to go. I slung my backpack into the Toyota Land Cruiser, hopped in the front passenger seat, and looked over at my driver. *I couldn't breathe.* I had an overpowering vision so real I could have sworn it was happening right then and there. I saw myself married to this man, living in Nicaragua, driving along dirt roads, sleeping in a small shack near the beach but nestled in the woods with two dogs, three horses, and children playing in the yard. I was so taken aback that I thought someone must have certainly drugged me, but I had had nothing to drink and was sober. All my senses had been engaged in that moment: the taste of his lips, the feeling of his skin, sleeping next to him, the children's laughter, the smell of the horses, and the feeling of driving down the bumpy dirt road.

I immediately realized Pablo did not speak English, resulting in the two-hour drive as a fun conversational type of charades. I handed him my business card and circled my email address as I stepped out of the truck at the airport, securing my backpack over my shoulder. He responded with a tight hug and a kiss on the cheek. It felt innocent and sweet, different from other men in the past. A hint of adventure was in this experience that made me feel alive, present, and connected.

The following day, an email from Pablo sat in my inbox. I eagerly opened it but could not read a single word. I had to copy and paste it into Google Translate: "Hi, this is your driver, Pablo. Nice to meet you. See the Sphinx in the stars with a turtle."

Huh? Confusion set in for a moment as I tried to process what his email meant. *Was he crazy?* I thought, and then I remembered that Google Translate did not always translate everything perfectly. I would definitely need to learn Spanish if I was going to invest in this relationship. I did not know how this would all work out, but I knew it was worth pursuing. That vision had been too strong to ignore.

CHAPTER 23

Dreams Do Come True

———————◆———————

A month later, I returned to Managua to reunite with Pablo. Our first date was in a safe location at a five-star hotel, and the staff spoke English. I had reserved a room for my stay, and we had lunch in the hotel restaurant. We used Google Translate on my iPad to communicate. I would speak into the iPad, the iPad would translate and repeat what I said in Spanish, and Pablo would do the same. It was probably quite comical for others in the restaurant to watch, but I did not care. We dined on pizza and wine. I was allowing myself to fall in love. By now, Nathan, at twenty-three, was living in his own apartment and working full-time. Gabriella was seventeen and starting her junior year of high school. My previous plan of pursuing a job with the National Transportation Safety Board (NTSB) and moving to Washington, DC, or relocating to Alaska, vanished without regret.

I continued flying and began commuting from Managua two months after I met Pablo. I would stay at his sister's small apartment because it was a short distance to the airport, and Pablo's cousin, Carlos, who was a taxi driver, could easily pick me up and drive me to Fidelia's home. The location made sense, and I scheduled my travel to maximize time with Pablo. But sometimes, due to my work schedule or flight availability, I flew in a few days earlier than planned. Fidelia's home was the perfect place to wait until Pablo could pick me up and take me to his village about an hour away on the Pacific Coast. As I walked out the door, I'd leave several twenty dollar bills tucked away for Fidelia as a thank-you for letting me stay in her home. The average income for Fidelia and most Nicaraguans was two hundred dollars a month.

Next to the kitchen, she had a small room set up for me with concrete walls and no windows. Howler monkeys often swung down into our open "kitchen" area where clothes were hung after being scrubbed on the washboard. The monkeys grabbed the fruit that had fallen on the floor from the mango tree branches that created shade in the kitchen. Often their sharp nails snagged clothing on the line, and I would find those items, such as socks and underwear, caught in the tree branches outside. Many times, I would awake to a rooster's *cock a doodle do* from underneath my bed. Scorpions and other insects crawled on the walls, making it necessary to slide the mattress away from the wall to avoid getting bit. I always slept with a hoodie over my head, socks on my feet, flip flops by the bed, and a low voltage night light to keep the room illuminated. No doubt, the family lived in poverty, but I loved them and accepted their living conditions.

The downside was that Managua was dangerous, especially for a white American female who didn't speak Spanish. I went outside to get air because of the stifling heat in the cramped house. There was no air conditioning, and the temperatures inside the concrete dwelling often crept up to over ninety degrees. Family members and friends created a circle around me so that the neighbors did not know when I was outside. They feared I would be attacked or robbed and wanted to protect me. When I was thirsty or hungry, I waited for Pablo's eleven-year-old niece, Maria, to come home from school. I gave her money, and she walked to the nearest corner store to buy me a cold beverage or snack.

Six months later, one part of the vision I had in the Land Cruiser came true. Pablo and I were married in a small quaint ceremony overlooking a steep mountainside outside of Managua. I had an interpreter and attorney present for the ceremony because I was not yet fluent in Spanish and wanted to make sure the ceremony and documents were legitimate. My family, horrified and convinced I had lost all common sense, did not attend the wedding in Nicaragua.

I was blessed to experience complete immersion within the country and community through unfiltered eyes with my new family. Doing so allowed me to witness the heartbreaking economic struggle of Nicaragua's societal deficit regarding education and other needs, along with the prevailing conditions of poverty.

I was inspired to help the community, so I combined my love of running with my love of education. During that time, I created my nonprofit: Runucate. I had no idea how to start a business and did not have the money to pay for an attorney or a company to walk me through the process. I have often had great ideas and leapt right in, not knowing exactly what steps to take but knowing my desired outcome. I preferred taking a sink-or-swim approach. I checked out books online, educated myself, and became familiar with the various roles and duties that needed to be maintained to successfully establish a nonprofit and dove in.

I committed to running in long-distance races to raise money for educational scholarships for all ages in Pablo's small village. I continued to commute between my work at Dulles Airport in Washington, DC, my home in Cleveland where my children lived, and Nicaragua where my husband was. I helped locals with English even though I had no formal English teaching certification. In the meantime, I was training for marathons on various continents to raise funds for the scholarships and grow the nonprofit I created.

Gabriella and Nathan were now older and self-sufficient and were rarely home. It was odd for me to be in Cleveland for more than a few days at a time.

CHAPTER 24

Severe Turbulence

———————◆———————

In a matter of months, my relationship with Pablo was tattered, and the cultural differences became discernible. The more Spanish I learned as I was living in Nicaragua, the more I realized that Pablo was not being honest with me on many levels, but I continued to doubt my suspicions. I helped him secure a tourist visa from the U.S. Embassy in April, four months into the marriage. I encouraged him to visit Cleveland to meet my children. I had been fully integrated into his family with his three adult children, five of his eleven siblings, numerous cousins, nieces, nephews, aunts, and uncles. It was time that he met my family and we blended our lives.

He absolutely lit up when he arrived in the United States for the first time. We enjoyed a week of relaxation, and I introduced him to all things American: hamburgers, pizza, hot dogs, bowling, and the 3D-IMAX theater. He had not expanded his English vocabulary beyond "yes," "I'm sorry," and "thank you." I had to accompany him, acting as a translator, every time he left the house. I was surprised that my neighbor Wendy let him ride her Harley Davidson around the neighborhood. She said he needed to have some fun and that the motorcycle had to be ridden and she could not do it because she had a shoulder injury. The bike had sat in her garage untouched for months. Pablo was eager to help. I told him to be back in ten minutes, but he was gone for an hour. Irritation turned to concern with each passing minute. When he returned, he was as excited as a child at Christmas. My heart soared with love for him, and I told myself we could overcome the cultural differences we had.

The tension with my friends and family began to ease after they met him, and our marriage now seemed great. His stay in Cleveland was short. Everyone was excited for him to return to the United States in the future.

The following month, I waited in my gynecologist's office after a routine exam and to refill my birth control pill prescription and was hit with shocking news. I was pregnant. It was a few weeks shy of my forty-first birthday. I had gotten pregnant when Pablo came to the United States. *How did this happen?* I had used contraception consistently for a decade. I did not know what to do and was not prepared to start a new family. Being surrounded by children had been part of my vision when I first sat next to Pablo in the truck at the resort, but the thought of pregnancy at my age terrified me. I was just getting my life together. I had become pregnant with Nathan at eighteen, and at this stage in my life, I was finding myself—my true self—and had the space to pursue my interests. One thing was certain—I was not going to go through a pregnancy in the uncomfortable conditions in Nicaragua.

Pregnancy in Nicaragua without my family and the familiar surroundings and comfort of the United States was not an option. Pablo needed to come to Ohio to not only help raise our child but also to work to supplement our income. I felt I had sacrificed and showed my devotion to the relationship. I had put in more effort by choice. I had lived in his country, learned Spanish, and given so much of myself. I now needed him to step up as a man and a father. Our circumstances had changed with the pregnancy, and I needed him. He still had not learned English, even though I had stressed the importance and necessity of doing so. I was certain the two of us could manage and perhaps have a great future. I convinced myself we would be a family of two cultures, traveling between countries and families, our lives rich and full.

It quickly became clear that continuing work as an airline pilot was no longer feasible with the stress of commuting and the lifestyle of the regional airlines. The realization created uncertainty. I didn't know if I could maintain my lifestyle standards or reach my goals. I allowed fear and pent-up emotions to bubble to the surface.

I sobbed uncontrollably for days with my neighbor Wendy. She had lived next door to me in Cleveland for fifteen years, and we had developed a tight connection. She had been through similar experiences: a divorce, single motherhood, financial struggles, abuse, etc. After several agonizing days, I knew what I had to do.

Wendy drove us to the clinic. Protesters lined the sidewalks with cardboard signs and horrific images. I was aware of the consequences and rationalized that I had not planned this pregnancy. I had not been irresponsible. I had been on birth control pills for nearly a decade, and I had shared my body with my husband, not with a random stranger. I felt awful as a maternal instinct kicked in and told me not to have an abortion. But I felt there was no other option. My children were in Hawaii with Jeff for his wedding. While he was getting married in paradise, I was lying in a sterile room, waiting for a doctor to sedate me days before my forty-first birthday.

I chose not to tell Pablo what I was doing because abortion was an unforgivable crime in his country. We had made arrangements for him to return to the United States and intended that he would become a resident because we were having a baby. My logic was to tell him after he arrived, but I never did.

Pablo's visa had not expired, and our plan was to ask for the tourism visa to be converted to a long-term visa. He arrived in Cleveland for the second time a few weeks later with two overstuffed duffel bags, ready to begin his new life. We had an appointment with an immigration attorney, Jennifer. She assured us obtaining a permanent visa would be no problem since we were married. She just needed to get the divorce documentation from Pablo's first marriage. Pablo told Jennifer he had been granted a special divorce with unique paperwork, but he did not have it. Jennifer seemed confused and asked how he married me in Nicaragua without the proper divorce decree. He just shrugged, avoided answering her directly, and said he would see what he could do.

As I walked out the door several steps behind Pablo, Jennifer motioned to me to wait. Even though Pablo did not speak English and would not have understood, she told me in hushed words, "I've never heard of a special divorce. Keep your eyes open."

Jennifer's warning stuck with me, and within a week, I grew suspicious. When he had arrived, I had given him a prepaid cell phone. I received a notification within three days from the carrier stating that the balance was zero. I checked the online account, certain the message was sent in error, but it was accurate. He was calling a Nicaraguan phone number when we were apart, usually when I was gone running errands or sleeping.

Late in the evening, I reloaded the cell phone, and holding my breath, dialed the number. "*Hola, mi amor. Te extraño,*" a husky voice seductively whispered. Her words meant, "Hello, my love. I miss you." I knew this well because I had said these exact words to Pablo many times in the past as the distance separated us.

My heart fell to the floor, and my stomach felt as if a punch had landed in the center. All the hurt of past relationships flooded back, the surreal feeling of this happening again.

In Spanish, I said, "This is Pablo's wife. Who is this?"

She rapidly spoke Spanish, and I could not understand much of what she said. She was using a lot of slang terms, and I could not grasp the full meaning of her words with my limited vocabulary. What I picked up was that she was pregnant. *Pregnant!* Pablo told her he was going to Boston to make money with his friend Larry to send to her and the baby. It *was* true that he had a friend Larry from Boston who lived in Nicaragua. He had covered for Pablo.

The realization hit me that I had brought a man into my home with my high school-aged daughter, had lost the respect of my family and many friends for this man, had given up a tremendous job opportunity, and had this man's child growing inside me—all while he was cheating on me and impregnating another woman. Our whole relationship—all of it—was a lie. My brain could not process this information, and I searched for a meaning that made sense while the woman on the other end screamed at me.

It was useless for me to attempt to have a conversation with her. The only way I could think to solve this was for her to speak directly to Pablo. So I asked her, "Do you want to speak with Pablo?" She promptly called me a liar and reminded me he was in Boston, the story he had told her.

"No, he's in Cleveland, in my bed. Let him tell you," I said as I made my way to the bedroom, my legs shaking with adrenaline.

I promptly went to the bedroom, iPhone in hand, on the speaker phone. I told him in Spanish that his pregnant girlfriend was on the phone and wanted to speak with him. He was startled and panicked, so he hung up. I redialed and pushed the speaker option again, and the two of them began to jabber in an unfamiliar dialect that was difficult for me to understand. She was crying, and I was busy shoving his belongings into the duffle bags he had brought to Cleveland, bags that still had the destination paper tags from the airlines attached to the handle. As I ripped them off, I calculated the dates and realized he had been sleeping with her before we got married and even after. She would have gotten pregnant the month we were wed.

When I drove him to the airport, he hesitantly got out of the car, stumbling over the yellow terminal curb. I hurled the prepaid cell phone at him, which shattered on impact with the concrete. It was three o'clock in the morning, no cars were in sight, and airport security was closed. I was throwing my new non-English speaking husband out. He pleaded with me because he did not have a ticket back to Managua. I didn't care; that was the least of my concerns now. *What am I going to do? My husband is returning to Nicaragua to be with a woman who is pregnant with his child. He lied to me. How long has he been lying? What else did he lie about? How am I going to face my family, coworkers, and neighbors? They are all going to tell me "I told you so."* Everything I thought I knew is a lie. I felt out of control, horrified, humiliated, betrayed, and lost.

In all the chaos and pain, relief lingered in the back of my mind. I did not know about the other woman in his life when I made the decision to have an abortion, but some of the stress was now alleviated. Even so, the shame, emotional pain, hurt, and horror of that decision weigh on me to this day. It was never an easy decision.

I had such a hard time coming to terms with my choice that I lied and told people, including my family, that I had a miscarriage. Everyone did not need to know the details, but I was fearful of their judgment, and I have not been able to bring myself to tell the truth about what had happened until now.

Pablo could figure out his own problems. I had no energy left to consider his feelings. If I did, I might have given him another chance because the fear of the unknown was more frightening than knowing what the future with him held. *With him gone, I have one fewer problem,* I thought. I reached out to the State Department days later and advised them of the situation. His visa was revoked with the help of an Ohio senator. It was time to put myself first.

CHAPTER 25

Starting Over Again

———————◆————————

I spent the next several months in a daze, heartbroken. My dreams of living in Nicaragua, teaching English, eating fresh mangoes, and listening to the sounds of the horses' hooves on the dirt road as they pulled carts were gone. Not only was I mourning the loss of our unborn child, but I was mourning the loss of a future with my husband. After months of paralysis, it was time to clean up the mess. I knew I needed to get a divorce from Pablo but not from Nicaragua.

It did not take long to figure out that the lies Pablo had told me were deeper than I had imagined. Pablo had still been married to a woman named Luisa when we married. They had been married for over fifteen years but were legally separated. The web had become more tangled than I imagined, and I knew I had to return to Nicaragua to not only tie up legal loose ends but to prove to myself that he did not break me. Despite all that I had just experienced, I couldn't shake the reality that the most important thing to me was helping others. If I had found any gift in Nicaragua, it was the discovery that giving back to a community and inspiring others was extremely gratifying. This allowed me to find fulfillment in something outside myself, something other than relationships and past negative patterns. Those things continued to disappoint me, but as I was able to actually give to someone and see their lives improve, I knew I had found something I couldn't just walk away from.

I arrived back in the Managua airport with a flood of emotions. During the long trip down, I had reflected on the decisions I had made and the reasons for them. As I looked back and became honest with myself, I realized that I had not made wise decisions nor had I used good judgment in many areas leading to this point.

At the realization of where I was in life, I began to slip into depression. I spent countless mornings talking myself into getting out of bed to face the day. I questioned my ability to make decisions. I wanted to be alone because it was less painful to be a recluse. That way, I did not have to see couples holding hands, sharing moments of connection, laughing. Each glance, smile, or kiss triggered gut-wrenching pain. I had stopped reading, one of my favorite pastimes, because I could not bear to read a paragraph about someone falling in love. Pablo's deception haunted me, and stacked with the previous betrayals of all the men in my life, I felt hopeless.

I researched becoming officially certified to teach English through a Teaching English as a Foreign Language (TEFL) program in León, a progressive college town on the west coast, an hour away from Pablo's village and Managua. As part of the program, I taught local students English.

I began to build a new life on my own and was proud of myself for having the strength to return to a country that now symbolized something very different for me: independence and confidence in myself. My Spanish was improving, and I was making friends with locals and expats. My closest friends and best resources were Samantha and Matt, Americans who had relocated to Nicaragua with their son and who had helped build the community and a successful English school and education program. They provided stability for me and a safe place to land emotionally while I navigated my turmoil of emotions.

Witnessing the impact that learning English had on a community was unlike anything I had ever experienced. The adult students would write me letters in English about the new opportunities because they could speak English. Opportunities included better working conditions with increased pay, the ability to send their children to school, and afford better medical care. The effort I put in equated to significant benefits for my students and their families. On a selfish note, it nurtured my soul and my desire to contribute for a greater good.

It was not easy trying to rebuild my life while my heart was fragmented into a thousand pieces. I commuted from Nicaragua to the United States as I worked as a pilot and searched for a way to grow my nonprofit, connect with others, contribute to the community and train for a marathon.

Despite the setbacks, I had several wins along the way. I successfully negotiated the rental terms in Spanish for an adorable apartment in a small *barrio* (neighborhood) outside of town a short drive from the beach. I had air conditioning, running water and a small kitchenette. I also had a tiled floor, an internet connection, a housekeeper, and a security guard. When I had been with Pablo at his home near the beach or in his sister's home in Managua, I had none of these things. At both locations, we had no running water, and the electricity was tapped into and shared by a dozen other homes, resulting in continuous blackouts. As a precaution, I learned to always keep a flashlight nearby when the lights went out to avoid an inadvertent run-in with a scorpion or a tarantula.

After much effort and time, at forty-two years old, I ran my first marathon (26.2 miles) in Ohio to support the mission of my nonprofit. I will admit that it was tough. I cried, ached, laughed, tripped, got up, and tripped again but kept going forward. Along the way, I discovered that running truly was a metaphor for life. I had always been told I was too curvy to run and that I did not have a runner's body, so I never tried. I never thought it was an option. But that day changed all that! Not only was I running, but I was helping lives as well. It was about what I believed could and should be done to help others in need and embrace life. I ran beyond my own self-imposed limits and the ones others had tried to set for me.

I connected with English teachers from all over the world and continued my philanthropy by running marathons globally. I was learning to stand on my own two feet, but my heart wrenched every time I thought of Pablo. I could not get him out of my mind, and then one day he contacted me. I had to ignore him because my heart was too fragile.

CHAPTER 26

Crooked Attorneys

———————◆———————

The attorneys I hired in Nicaragua to end my illegal marriage were licensed and highly recommended. But many locals believed the misconception that all Americans had abundant wealth. They thought this as well and took financial advantage of me regarding what they charged for their legal representation. I had been willing to pay the agreed-upon fee, but one day, when I was in their home office, they told me the fee had more than doubled with no explanation. I questioned the increase, and they said we would discuss it over dinner and offered to give me a ride to my apartment. It was getting late, and walking in the dark was not a smart idea. Normally, I would have taken a taxi, but I agreed as I wanted to continue the discussion.

Instead of driving to a restaurant, they drove me to an ATM to pay up. When I saw the shiny blade of a machete sitting on the driver's lap, their intentions were clear if I didn't oblige. I was to withdraw as much cash as the ATM would allow and give it to them in exchange for a safe ride back to my apartment and so that I would not be abandoned in the late evening in an unsafe neighborhood. The only reasonable assumption was that they would have used the machete on me, a common weapon of choice in Nicaragua. The machine let me withdraw three hundred dollars from one bank card and two hundred from another card before the ATM ran out of cash. I silently thanked the universe for the lack of available funds. Discouraged, they left me standing alone in front of the machine, still five blocks from my apartment. Fat rain drops splashed across my face, soaking my bag full of legal documents as I rushed through the deserted streets, hoping that no one lurked in the dark shadows.

After that—broken, scared, and emotionally drained—I gave up. I could not keep up the fight any longer. I went to the most familiar place I knew, even if it was toxic. I responded to one of the many messages Pablo had sent me, and we reignited our love affair using a skill I'd perfected my entire life. I compartmentalized the pain. I had never told him I had an abortion and let him believe I had a miscarriage. I avoided the subject whenever possible. When I was in Nicaragua, Pablo would visit my apartment for short periods of time because he needed to return to his new baby and girlfriend. She could not know he was seeing me again.

I had become the other woman. But our relationship was never the same as trust had been severed that night in Cleveland. The same voice that spoke to me over the years that encouraged me to take flying lessons, to be more than I thought imaginable, to stand up for myself, had been silenced. I let insecurity and fear guide my choices. I knew I had to stop seeing Pablo and leave Nicaragua, but the thought of what the future held terrified me.

UNITED STATES— JOURNEY HOME

CHAPTER 27

Signs from the Universe

———————————◆———————————

Political unrest broke out in Nicaragua in April 2018 after a series of protests against a tax increase by President Ortega. The citizens of Nicaragua responded with a series of peaceful protests that turned violent when the government became aggressive in its efforts to break up and quash them. The people retaliated, and in a matter of days, the situation became very unstable and scary. University students barricaded themselves inside of classrooms, snipers shot innocent people, and road pavers were ripped up to block off streets and used as a shield against Molotov cocktails. The situation became dire as citizens resorted to using handmade slingshots to protect themselves as the United Nations declared human rights violations against the government. The U.S. Embassy was evacuating non-essential personnel. People were burning tires in the streets as I drove by, often unable to get to the airport because of closed streets and continued danger. Most flights into Managua were canceled until the situation was more certain.

It took these signs to show me it was time to change directions—to leave Nicaragua and to leave Pablo. I had revoked his visa, which would more than likely prevent him from ever entering the United States legally, and I knew I was shutting the door on our relationship permanently. The last time I saw him, we spent the weekend at a small hotel in Poneloya on the beach. I knew it was the last time I would see Pablo. But he had no idea. I tried to take in every moment—the smells, the tastes, the laughter—and hoped I could etch the memories inside my brain. I was soaking up all Nicaragua offered before I took my last flight back home to Cleveland. Two days later, I returned to Ohio, leaving behind my scholarship program, friends, a home, and so much more. The change was devastating but provided yet another opportunity to reinvent myself and helped me to understand that what we think is a problem is really a gift if we change our perspective.

It's hard to remember, but for weeks or perhaps months after I returned to the United States, I was in a familiar place of emptiness, solitude, and heartbreak as I questioned why I wasn't good enough. I had done all the right things and made myself available physically and emotionally but had somehow still been betrayed, blinded by my naivety. I knew the only way to get myself out of this negative mental state was to put the focus back on giving good back to the world. I had fallen in love with serving others in Nicaragua as I saw the hope in their eyes, the smiles on their faces, and their determination to make a better life. Witnessing these transformations infused me with love, purpose, and connection. I had previously been living for a cause greater than myself and knew I had to find a way to feel that again.

Pablo and I spoke a handful of times in the months after my departure about the possibility of his return to the United States because the situation had become dire for him. He failed to understand that the consequences of his past behavior and the revocation of his visa had resulted in permanent denial into the United States. I consulted with an attorney in Cleveland about acquiring a divorce. But the marriage had not been registered domestically, and since he was still legally married to someone else, the marriage was not valid. This was a bittersweet victory. The last communication I received from him was months later. He was trying to cross the border as a refugee into Costa Rica to seek safety and employment.

CHAPTER 28

A New Mission

———————◆———————

Not long after returning to Ohio, I was passing through the airport in Cleveland on my way to work. I stopped inside the United Club, a lounge for traveling passengers that provided a paid yet quiet space to escape the loud and busy terminal with food and beverages. As I was getting a cup of coffee from the dispenser, a woman was wiping down the counter next to me. We struck up a conversation and she introduced herself as Margo. She shared with me that she not only worked in the United Club but also volunteered as a tutor at a local nonprofit organization. The school offered test preparation for adult learners through a variety of programs and educational tools to help students break a root cause of poverty: illiteracy.

Margo told amazing stories about the GED students she worked with and how proud she was of them. She said that so many lacked confidence and direction stemming from abuse. I had been one of those students and still was. I was continuing to run away from my past and trying to break the chains of a lifetime of abuse, depression, and fear.

Right then, I connected the dots, and a shift rumbled deep inside my soul. In that moment of clarity, I understood why I had hidden my story, hidden my past. Not only had I been hiding it from others, but I had also hidden it from myself. The focus had been on fear—the fear of being judged, being rejected, seen as a victim, being found out, being an imposter, and not being good enough. But I realized then that all the experiences from the past had made me into who I was today and who I was becoming.

Everyone has fear, and it was time to face mine, own my story, and stop letting my story own me. I had to begin to share the real me because everyone has their own journey, but so many of us turn our story into a nightmare. We turn it into a tale of despair instead of using it to empower ourselves and others. So often it becomes what destroys us instead of what equips us to move forward. People are amazing and have unlimited potential if they do not let fear sit in the driver's seat.

Margo connected me with the organization she volunteered at, and I agreed to speak with their GED class at both their locations. The session was going to be a round-table discussion, and I would share my experiences and then answer questions from the students.

As I walked into the classroom, I did not know what I would say, but I did not let fear lead. Many of the students greeted me with excited recognition. "Hey, you're the lady that ran with lions!" Katie, the marketing manager, had hyped the announcements for my talk. She highlighted a marathon I had run the previous year during an African safari as a marketing tactic for a scholarship fundraiser. She focused on the wild game, such as zebras, hippos, wildebeests, and crocodiles I had encountered, emphasizing the lions. It was true to a certain extent, but the rangers in the conservatory had made sure the lions were far enough away that they were not a threat to the runners. Many thought of me as this exotic, adventurous woman, and they were correct. But what they did not know yet was that I struggled with many of the same things they did. I knew one thing with certainty: these learners wanted to hear about lions.

This was the first time I would share intimate life details publicly: the abuse, dropping out of high school, the unplanned pregnancies, the alcohol use, the heartbreak with men, the failure to leave bad relationships, feeling like an imposter, triumph, fear, and despair. The more I shared, the more connected I felt with these students, and the stronger I became. I knew this was my new path. At times, I seemed to just be sharing another story, but to them, it was more than that. It was proof that they could also change their lives and that what they struggled with was normal and could be overcome.

I made the decision to resurrect my nonprofit, and partner with this organization to raise awareness and funds for adult education and to fight illiteracy. It felt right. The best way to do this was to commit to run a marathon on all seven continents. I took the approach that I had used in Nicaragua for the scholarship program of running marathons. This shift felt closer to home because I had been exactly where they were. I had been the one who others doubted and cast to the side because I had too many struggles: single parenthood, financial issues, a history of abuse, and more. Had I had a role model or a sense of community when I was younger, I might have changed my situation sooner. I knew it was important to stand up and be a leader and be that person to someone else.

I held the first marathon fundraiser for a race in Southeast Asia in November 2018 in Myanmar (formerly Burma) called the Bagan Temple Marathon. I was excited and so were the students. During my marathon training, I remembered the way the students faces lit up when they thought about their future and knew they had the control to make a difference. This kept me moving forward on days when I felt overwhelmed. Not only had I been motivating them, but they were encouraging me and giving me the strength to move forward too.

The next marathon I committed to run was in June 2019 on the most remote inhabited island in the world—Easter Island. It was isolated in the Pacific Ocean nearly twenty-three hundred miles west of South America and eleven hundred miles from the nearest island. The students loved the exotic locations and hearing stories about what I was doing.

The connection during my speaking sessions was so strong that the director asked me to give the GED graduation commencement speech in June 2019. I eagerly accepted. However, I felt a lot of pressure because the previous year's speaker was a senator. I had spoken in front of thirty students but had estimated that more than one hundred people, including the family members, would attend. I was intimidated, but I kept remembering I was bringing them value and recognition because they had come so far. I was there to cheer them on and to encourage them to keep going. I emphasized Zig Ziglar's approach to life: "There is no elevator to success, you have to take the stairs."[1] You have to do the work to achieve success in anything you do.

During the speech, I started to cry and tried desperately to keep the tears from flowing and my voice from cracking. My eyes locked in on Katie's in an attempt to maintain my composure. I was caught up with emotion when I spoke about the labels we place on ourselves that cover who we truly are. I had placed all kinds of labels on myself: high school dropout, stripper, victim, single mom, loser, and many more. After the speech, when I was talking with the graduates, many of the staff and family members told me they fought back tears as well. No one cared how perfect my words were, but what they did care about was my authenticity and transparency as I shared.

1 "No Elevator to Success", Ziglar.com, https://www.ziglar.com/quotes/ success-and-failure/, accessed March 12, 2020.

CHAPTER 29

Owning My Story

———◆———

The local speaking I did in Cleveland gained the attention of an international nonprofit group that promotes adult literacy through content development, programs and advocacy, ProLiteracy. They read an article about my contribution to the GED students in a newsletter, which led them to want to learn more. The marketing director, Michele, reached out to me to see if I was interested in being the keynote speaker at their bi-annual event in San Diego in five months. The estimated attendance was one thousand people. I froze on the other end of the phone. In my mind, I started doubting the validity of the offer.

Does she have the right Courtney Schoch? I thought. *Does this woman realize I have no professional speaking experience?* was the next question I asked myself as Michele continued to tell me what the compensation was. *They will pay me to tell my story? What's the catch?* This thought quickly followed the others. I knew my story inspired people, but I never considered to what extent or that I could be financially compensated.

As soon as I hung up, I called my mom. "Mom, an organization just asked me to be their speaker at a large conference. They are going to pay me a lot of money and . . ." My voice trailed off. I tried not to cry and held back tears; my vision blurred, and the lump in my throat grew larger. I continued, "They want me to tell my story because it will inspire people." This was the first time in my life that I felt I had true value to deliver on a large scale. I realized this opportunity would not only give me courage but also hope that it would inspire others. I stepped outside my comfort zone and pushed fear aside and accepted the invitation.

The introduction video that ProLiteracy shot when they came to Washington Dulles Airport played before I walked on the stage, and in less than two minutes, my mind went blank. I took several deep breaths to recenter myself as I remembered the wise advice of a singer I knew, who had a terrible fear of performing. She said that she would become nervous, but she quickly learned that the physical cues that indicate fear are the same as the ones that indicate excitement, so we simply have to choose which one we want it to be. Fast breathing, butterflies in the stomach, tense shoulders, and an uncertain feeling about what will happen next are all indicators of both. The difference is the language we use to describe the feelings. I made the mental shift to excitement and confidently strode to the stage, my dress swishing lightly with each step.

As soon as I began speaking, index cards in hand in case I forgot what to say, I knew I was meant to do this. All the nervousness disappeared, and I spoke from my heart to each person seated in the audience. I understood that every person—not just me—has a powerful story. What we do with our story makes the difference, and by owning our story and our experiences, we become the captain of our destiny. We decide on the destination and how we direct our energy along the journey. If the focus is on negativity and drama, that is where our attention and impact will be greatest, taking us off our desired course.

After I finished speaking and walked down the stage stairs, I felt the love and energy from the room. I was confident in myself and so grateful to those who had faith in me and gave me the opportunity to inspire all these people. So many of them approached me afterward and shared their stories, personal and intimate accounts of triumphs and tragedies. They had wide smiles on their faces or tears sliding over their cheeks. That day, I learned how to show up for myself and others to make a difference.

CHAPTER 30

The Next Big Win

——————————◆——————————

The next big win was when I received an unexpected call from Lancôme. They are a part of the L'Oréal Luxury Products division and provide upscale skin care, fragrances, and makeup worldwide. They asked me to be their inspirational speaker the following month in Manhattan at the United States headquarters. They planned a Day of Giving for forty adult learners that included style makeovers. They timed it so that many of the industry's top hairstylists and makeup artists were in town. They had agreed to donate their time and talent to make this event a success. I would have an hour to share my story and inspire those in attendance, a total of approximately one hundred people gathered in an intimate setting.

When I arrived at the building in Hudson Yards, I was warmly welcomed. They took me to the thirty-sixth floor and whisked me away to have my hair and makeup done. I felt like a movie star, a VIP, a feeling I had never experienced. After hair and makeup, I had my photos professionally taken. Hotels and travel started to have a different meaning to me than what I experienced at the airlines.

After a social with a creative array of appetizers and beverages overlooking the Hudson River and Manhattan, it was time for me to take the stage. An area had been set up for me at the front of the large meeting space paneled by full glass and an incredible balcony.

I feared I would not connect with the audience in New York. I thought my story had only been well received in San Diego because the attendees were there for a conference on adult education and related topics, so that was their area of interest. In contrast, this group consisted of adult learners but also of many professionals with no ties to that field or those who did not know much about the subject. Would I be able to deliver value to them? Even so, I had confidence that what I was about to share would impact them and connect with them on a human level. Fear is universal, regardless of circumstances, and the way we use fear is important. When it's used productively, it can take us to new levels.

I had plenty of time to connect with the audience, and this time, unlike in San Diego, I veered from my script and gave the people what I felt they needed. One attendee wrote a review and described the audience attentiveness when I had the microphone. In her words, "You could have heard a pin drop." I spoke from the heart, and when the floor opened up for answers, the questions poured in. I walked around handing the microphone to people so others could hear them.

"How were you able to forgive those who hurt you? Especially some of the people that did such terrible things to you? How can I forgive others?" a gentleman asked me.

I realized that people are doing the best that they can. "Forgiving is more about allowing ourselves to move on and for our benefit. Living in anger and hurt prevents us from living our lives with passion. In a sense, we continue to give control to the person who hurt us, and by not forgiving, we allow the action to continue to hurt us long after the event has passed," I explained.

"What do you do to get you through the tough times? Do you have daily rituals?" a woman questioned.

"I remind myself that I've been through tough times before and I've come out stronger on the other side of those difficulties. You can't appreciate the good times if you do not know what the not-so-good times feel like. The struggles allow me to have a deeper understanding of myself and life. To grow. They allow me the ability to connect to others."

"Daily rituals or actions I commit to are meditation, a clean diet, exercise, minimal alcohol consumption, mindfulness, write in my journal, perform a minimum of three acts of selfless kindness, and set clear intentions. Doing any or all of these things will improve your life and help you gain clarity and move you forward."

"How do you handle fear now?" a young lady quietly asked.

"It took me a long time to realize that fear is healthy if it is used correctly. It's here to protect us, but sometimes we have to tell it to sit in the backseat and not in the driver's seat. When I am scared or uncertain of doing something, I pause and ask myself, 'What is this fear really about?' For example, am I fearful because I'm about to do something new? Am I afraid of being rejected or looking stupid? Do I think I am going to experience a loss? Am I afraid of what people will think? I answer the questions honestly, and if the action is not going to hurt me or someone else, I typically choose to mindfully move forward. I tap into the strength I know I have. I let that strong, wise Courtney sit in the driver's seat, and then I push the gas pedal. Action creates confidence and growth."

The story I share not only applies to adult learners but resonates on some level with almost everyone, regardless of their background. The conversations I've had and the experiences I've shared have taught me that many of us are searching for guidance and connection. Humans struggle with life in general. But without challenges, we do not grow, and without growth, we stagnate and become unhappy. Self-doubt often sits front and center, acting as a barricade to the road forward. Our past is not our future. We learn from our past so that we can make our future brighter. We will always face challenges, and how we respond shapes our future.

SECTION FIVE
NEXT DESTINATION—
UNKNOWN

CHAPTER 31

Sky's the Limit

———————◆———————

I returned to flying, but nearly every day was a struggle. I knew I had outgrown my current position as a captain several months—if not years—earlier. The job no longer stimulated me and I was worn out. Late flights, angry passengers, broken airplanes, weather delays, demanding schedules—these were all a cumulative struggle that depleted my energy levels and made me question the longevity of my career.

When I lived in Nicaragua, I looked for a way to serve others and used the TEFL certification as my vehicle to give back. Flying airplanes was exciting, challenging, and met my need for significance, but it no longer fulfilled those needs. I only slept in my home six or seven days a month and was disconnected from my family and friends. My house had fallen into disrepair due to my hectic schedule. My time did not belong to me. The regional airlines had become more demanding with increased flight hours because of the pilot shortage as management implemented mandatory extensions that impacted not only my nonprofit and speaking engagements but also my health. Chronic fatigue set in as I suffered from poor sleeping patterns.

The universe sent several incidents or, as I like to believe, signs my way. Now twenty-six, my son became seriously ill while on vacation in Italy. He contracted an unknown bacterial virus that attacked his liver, and he lost a significant amount of weight within a few months of the trip. Constant visits to the doctor in an attempt to identify and find a course of treatment took a toll on him and the family. Next, my mother's health began to fail as well with a series of illnesses that also required hospital stays. Both these situations demanded my attention, and I asked work for a leave of absence so that I could regroup.

I felt as if I were burning a candle at both ends, or as if I were a house of cards waiting to collapse, and I was the only card the others balanced on. My memory had begun to falter, and I worried that I was no longer fit for flight duty because management was pushing me too hard to complete flights without the energy reserves to do so. I still hesitated because I doubted that I could handle the tremendous amount of financial responsibility I had.

If I left my position, even for a short period of time, the potential for financial disaster would significantly increase. I was fixated on all I would lose—not what I could gain—if I made changes.

Then the universe stepped in and gave me one huge shove in the direction I needed to go that I didn't see coming. My daughter, away at college in her third year, began suffering panic attacks and was diagnosed with a severe eating disorder. She needed to be admitted into a residential rehabilitation facility immediately. There was no other option. It was time to be home with my family, the family I loved and missed from years of traveling.

My mother's words echoed in my mind: "Families stick together, no matter what." But this time, I heard the phrase in another context, one with meaning and love. This time, the decision to stick together was not one of obligation but one of choice.

A friend once said to me nearly twenty years ago, "Courtney, do you know why you keep so busy all the time? It's so you don't have to stop and think. You have not processed some things inside your head yet, and if you keep going, you don't have to. You're going to burn out one day and be forced to slow down." That friend was correct.

I was running from all the things I had compartmentalized over the years, and when I faced them, my life changed forever. The thought of leaving the skies invoked the fear of loss, the fear of change, and the fear of financial demise. But instead of focusing on what could go wrong, I decided to focus on what could go right. I asked better questions to change my life. That was exactly what I had done nearly two decades earlier when I was in a loveless marriage and took my first flight lesson. I asked better questions, and I *did* change my life. When circumstances change and situations no longer serve us, we need to reevaluate and make course corrections as necessary. Making a decision and putting a plan of action into motion creates confidence to keep moving forward.

I'm traveling a new route now of designing my life with the skills I've acquired through experience. Yes, there is fear, so every day, I start by asking myself a simple question: *What am I afraid of?* The answer is not complicated. I am afraid of the unknown.

I then implement the same advice I gave to the audience in Manhattan. I ask myself a series of questions and step into curiosity instead of criticism: *What am I grateful for? What am I excited about? Where do I want to go? Why do I want to go there? What is this really about? How do I define failure for this? Could I possibly succeed? What if things went right? How can I contribute in a meaningful way?* The objective is clear: I want to inspire others to live their best lives, and I intend to create a supportive community that promotes change. This is my passion. My life's mission is to teach and lead while inspiring growth and discovery in myself and others. I believe life's challenges are opportunities for reinvention and welcome the unknown path that lies ahead.

Every day, I find a way to own my story and not let it own me. I could have easily continued to identify as a victim or beat myself up for not making better decisions. But each event has shaped me into who I am now. History is a series of events, and we cannot change the past: what we can change is the meaning we give events. The meaning we give our past can empower or destroy us. Only you have the power to decide. So why not focus on what's right instead of what's wrong, and give yourself permission to live the life you deserve?

The future is uncertain, but as your captain I want to share my fundamental belief about life; It's not about what you get during the journey; it's about who you become along the way. You should never settle for less than you can be and always be more than you thought possible.

This is your captain speaking. I look forward to seeing you at the next destination.

Lightning Source UK Ltd.
Milton Keynes UK
UKHW040655050922
408358UK00001B/368

9 781734 893540